"Denis Waitley cares about you and wants you to win at life."

—Kenneth Blanchard, Ph.D.
Coauthor of *The One Minute Manager*

"Success, both inner and outer, is our birthright, and Dr. Waitley shows us how."

—Harold H. Bloomfield, M.D.
Psychiatrist and Author

"From the day I met Dr. Waitley, he has been my source of inspiration, and I feel honored to be included in his book. In my sad or low moments, I think of Dr. Denis Waitley, and I smile."

—Wilma Rudolph, President
Wilma Rudolph Foundation,
Olympic Gold Medal Winner

"Dr. Denis Waitley knows the ingredients of true success and how to communicate this knowledge. I think of him as one of the really top motivational psychologists that we have today anywhere in the world."

—Dr. Charles Allen, Pastor
First United Methodist
Church, Houston, Texas

"In these days, we need the sound counsel of author Denis Waitley."

Ted W. Engstrom, President
World Vision

"Dr. Waitley is saying something that is new—perceptive—terribly _____ explosive in power

Berkley books by Dr. Denis Waitley

THE PSYCHOLOGY OF WINNING
THE WINNER'S EDGE

The Psychology Of Winning

Dr. Denis Waitley

BERKLEY BOOKS, NEW YORK

This Berkley book contains the complete
text of the original hardcover edition.
It has been completely reset in a typeface
designed for easy reading, and was printed
from new film.

THE PSYCHOLOGY OF WINNING

A Berkley Book / published by arrangement with
Nightingale-Conant Corporation

PRINTING HISTORY
Nightingale-Conant edition published 1979
Berkley edition / May 1984
Fifth printing / February 1985
Sixth printing / July 1985

ISBN: 0-425-08377-2

A BERKLEY BOOK ® TM 757.375
Berkley Books are published by The Berkley Publishing Group,
200 Madison Avenue, New York, New York 10016.
The name "BERKLEY" and the stylized "B" with design
are trademarks belonging to Berkley Publishing Corporation.
PRINTED IN THE UNITED STATES OF AMERICA

SPECIAL ACKNOWLEDGMENT

I would like to thank Dr. Jonas Salk, who has been an inspiration in my professional and personal life. His wisdom, dedication, compassion, and optimism are unmatched in any other individual I have had the privilege to consider a friend.

When I think of Jonas Salk, I think of life and health rather than disease and cure. He has taught me the real meaning of the Win-Win possibilities to Order in the Universe. Because of him I will always thirst for truth and wisdom.

ACKNOWLEDGMENTS

Dr. Jonas Salk

Dr. Hans Selye

Dr. Abraham Maslow

Earl Nightingale

Dr. Maxwell Maltz

James Newman

Dr. William Glasser

Dr. Viktor Frankl

Anne Morrow Lindbergh

Dr. Carl Rodgers

Lloyd Conant

Margaret Mead

Dr. Robert Eliot

Dr. Georgi Lozanov

Samuel Long

DEDICATION

To my parents...
who have made me feel special

To my children...
who make living a joyous happening

To Susan...
who makes every day a homecoming

And in memory of my beloved grandmother,
Mabel Reynolds Ostrander,
who taught me all there is about beauty,
love and human grace.

FOREWORD

Jonestown, the weird occult, sexual aberration, violence, crime, mysticism, drugs, escapism, purposelessness, indulgence, apathy, human indignity, greed, terrorism, obscenity...previews of the 1980's?

Books, movies, television, magazines, newspapers, protests, parties, lifestyles...all bombard us with stark brutality alluding to the new "realism" in our society.

What is "realism" but an illusion of reality? Investigative reporting has brought a new system of checks and balances, and social conscience to the leadership of the nation. However, beyond the factual revelation of the ills of society— in order that it might be improved—there is an alarming focus in every medium of human expression today on deviant behavior and the acts of a mentally deranged minority in the world.

So powerful and frequent are the slick, dramatic portrayals of the most revolting human biographies that society is methodically being transformed by example into a working model for *Losers.*

If one should dare revolt against the "revolting," he or she is immediately branded as naive, Pollyanna, a religious zealot, or out of touch with the times. If there's not enough violence, perversion or porno...it won't move the masses, sell tickets or gain ratings any more.

For me, since life is a brief journey, I will not waste it joining the thundering herd who worship the golden calf, the four-letter word, group "swing" or some Utopian cult approaching the twenty-first century, bored with all but the sensational, the morbid and the sickening...as if the decay and destruction of ancient civilizations from social cancer served no purpose in history but to preview the ever-predictable "Losing Cycle" of coming human attractions.

We need not always lose and fall—Egyptians, Mayans, Greeks, Romans, and Americans. Life is a fantasy of our own imagination. It can be a living nightmare or a living miracle...a Hell or Heaven on Earth!

For me, I prefer flowers over weeds—and natural beauty over invented placebo. I'll pass the substitute euphoria of pot and coke, uppers and downers...for a walk near the tidal pools, a romp with kids and dogs, a sunset, a hang glider, and a two-mile jog at dawn. I will always love and cherish life.

For me, there is only time enough to Win...

but no time at all to Lose!

THIS BOOK IS DIRECTED AND OFFERED TO THE READER WHO IS MORE INTERESTED IN MENTAL HEALTH THAN IN MENTAL ILLNESS...IN GROWTH THAN IN APATHY...IN WINNING THAN IN LOS-ING.

TABLE OF CONTENTS

The
Psychology
Of
Winning

OVERVIEW

The Game of Life: The Winners' Circle

P. O. W.

PRISONER OF WAR?
PRINCE OF WALES?
POWER OF WOMEN?
PRISONER OF WISHES?
PSYCHOLOGY OF WINNING!

THE WINNERS' CIRCLE

What could an undernourished black youth on the streets of San Francisco expect, especially since he was suffering from a crippling disease associated with malnutrition called rickets, which made his legs scrawny, weak and bowed? He was given encouragement and leg braces. Not much of a head-start program!

And yet, this kid with the funny legs and the funny first name somehow developed an incurable case of "The Psychology of Winning." When he was eleven years old, he attended a banquet honoring the legendary NFL running back, Jim Brown.

"I'll break every record you set," the youngster promised Brown.

The kid with the funny legs has since shortened his funny first name because his name is seen and used so much today. You may not remember little Orenthal, but you are certain to recognize the great O.J. . . . . running the length of the NFL football fields with blazing speed and incredible balance, setting all-time rushing records and running through airports renting cars on TV . . . running, all the way to the bank and into sports history!

You are either the captive or the captain of your thoughts. You can resign yourself to mediocrity or you can dare to dream of conquering outer space, inspiring the youth of our nation, discovering a cure for a dread disease, helping the less fortunate, creating a new masterpiece of art or music, or even of changing history.

Is it foolish to dream of being the first woman president? Golda Meir didn't think so. Foolish to imagine standing on the moon? Neil Armstrong dared to imagine.

Certainly one of the most challenging of all the great maxims to come from the lips and pens of history's teachers has been interpreted as the "strangest secret" by Earl Nightingale, one of our most respected broadcasters and writers:

"The fact that we, literally, become what we think about most of the time."

This declaration touches all of us without discrimination. The promise is the same for the inquisitive youth, the ambitious man or woman, the nurturant mother... Oriental or Occidental, Black or White, Chicano or Indian, Islamic or Christian. As you see yourself in the heart of your thoughts— in your mind's eye—so you do become!

Neil Armstrong's vision began as a child. In an interview immediately following his historic first step on the moon, he said: "Ever since I was a little boy, I dreamed that I would do something important in aviation."

It is fascinating that the thoughts of a child can shape a destiny so dramatically that this particular youth was to grow up to make the most significant footprints on the sands of time of any aviator during the first century of man's flight.

What you "see" in your mind's eye is what you get. Alcoholic or athlete—prostitute or nurse—drug pusher or teacher—nobody or somebody—loser or winner. Each of us becomes that make-believe self that we have imagined and fantasized most.

P.O.W. TAKES ON A NEW MEANING

Not too long ago, the letters P.O.W. on an automobile bumper sticker stood for "Prisoner of War" and the message elicited a response of conscience, sorrow or patriotism. A student at Oxford, however, is likely to use the same three letters to refer to the Prince of Wales, and with different emotional overtones. And feminine activists are likely to be seen carrying placards bearing the same three letters. To them, P.O.W. means Power of Women, and, of course, the emotional overtones are much different.

Three little letters charged with a kaleidoscope of emotions, depending upon one's experiences and attitudes. Life is uniquely individual through the eyes of each beholder. Any given event will elicit a positive, negative or neutral response, depending on the particular frame of reference of the observer.

Since we can choose our attitudes, let us expunge the negative connotations from the letters P.O.W. and assign to them the new meaning... "Psychology of Winning." The individual who understands the principles of winning in life, and who can apply those principles to benefit himself or herself and loved ones is bound to feel good, think constructively, look great, and expect the best.

The most important single point in the chapters to follow, to remember and internalize, is that *it makes little difference what is actually happening, it's how you, personally, take it that really counts!*

Examining the Psychology of Winning, we can compare life to a game, but it's not like football, for instance. In life there are no time-outs, no substitutions and the clock is always running.

Some people still think life is a practice game with the "big play" or Superbowl coming up at the end of the season.

Only after years have slipped away do they realize that they were inextricably involved in the "big game" every day of their lives.

Although there are no replays and your dreams may be intercepted or sacked again and again, there is one encouraging fact about this earnest game of life... and that's the fact that the real loss or win need not be decided until the final gun, if you consider there is ever a final gun in life.

It's startling how fast the first half of this game of life goes. The young man of thirty-five is sobered by the thought that he already has lived half of his allotted "three score years and ten." He winces when he watches his teenage son get racked up on the football field, then remembers that it was only yesterday that his father agonized for him. He attends open house at the high school with his daughter and is amazed at how much the teachers have changed since they taught him. He banters with his English teacher, now white-haired, and says "You sure look older, Mr. Clark." And he has to swallow as the teacher retorts, "So do you Denis—I hardly recognized you!"

When Omar Khayyam, in his classic poem *The Rubaiyat*, compared time with a bird on the wing, it is doubtful if even he realized just how fast the Bird of Time flies. Surely Jonathan Livingston Seagull in his finest form could not speed nearly as fast!

It behooves all of us concerned with the value of time to relish it... to savor every moment as though it were a vintage wine to sip or a double rainbow. And whether you are in the opening minutes of the Game of Life, or in any of the remaining three quarters... determine once and for all that you'll play the game to win.

THERE IS NO TIME TO LOSE!

There are three types of people involved in the game of life:

First, there are the Spectators. They are the majority who watch life happen as bystanders. They avoid the main arena for fear of being rejected, ridiculed, hurt, or defeated. They prefer not to make waves or get involved and would rather watch it happen on television. Most of all, the spectators in life fear winning. It's not losing they fear most...it's the possibility of winning! After all, winning carries the burden of responsibility and for setting a good example. That's too much of an effort for most. And so they watch others do their thing.

Next, there is another large mass of humanity called the Losers. By Losers, we do not refer to the millions of hungry and destitute throughout the world. The Losers we are speaking of are the people in our abundant society, here in this country, who never win...for they would rather look like...dress like...have fun like...earn like...have a house like...act like...or be...someone else. You can always spot Losers by the way they envy or criticize others...after all, misery loves company. Most of all, you can spot Losers by the way they put themselves down.

Then, there are the Winners. These are the few who in a very natural, free-flowing way seem to get what they want from life. They put themselves together across the board— at work, at home, in the community, and in society. They set and achieve goals which benefit themselves and others.

The term "Winning" may sound phony to you. Too materialistic. Too full of A's, or luck, or odds, or muscle-bound athletes.

True Winning, however, is no more than one's own personal pursuit of individual excellence. You don't have to get lucky to win at life, nor do you have to knock other people down or gain at the expense of others.

"Winning" is taking the talent or potential you were born with, and have since developed, and using it fully toward a goal or purpose that makes you happy.

Winning is becoming that dream of yourself that would fulfill you as a person with high self-esteem.

Winning is giving and getting in an atmosphere of love,

cooperation, social concern, and responsibility.

Winning is coming in fourth, exhausted and encouraged—because last time you came in fifth.

Winning is giving yourself to others freely.

Winning is never whining.

Winning is treating animals like people and people like brothers and sisters.

Winning is turning all the cards up in solitaire—without cheating.

Winning is picking up a beer can you didn't throw on the beach.

Winning is being glad you are you.

Winning is habit forming. (So is Losing.)

Winning is unconditional love.

Winning is a way of thinking—a way of living.

Winning is all in the attitude!

Talent is cheap. You can buy it, and recruit it. It's everywhere. The world is full of talented alcoholics.

Education is not cheap, but it's for sale and for hire if you have the time and money. You can get your BS, MBA or PhD. You can panel your den with diplomas. But the world is full of educated derelicts, unable to relate to supportive roles with others.

Not aptitude . . . *attitude* is the criterion for success. But you can't buy an attitude for a million dollars. Attitudes are not for sale.

All individuals are not born equal. Some are cursed and some are blessed with their hereditary uniforms. Equality is not Nature's way. The equal right to become unequal by choice is the natural cycle.

All environments do not breed and nurture the winning spirit. And yet, how often we are witness to living examples of greatness springing out of adversity.

How many Winners there are in the game of life who have rejected their genetic handicap and walked out of an environmental ghetto into a new world where self-esteem and the esteem of others abounds.

Attitude is the answer.

Your *attitude* toward your potential is either the key to or the lock on the door of personal fulfillment.

There are three main arenas in which you play your game of life. They are full of interaction. They are neither separate nor independent. Each is full of opportunities to use more of your vast, untapped potential.

In Losers, they can be likened to a "three-ring-circus" where too many confused activities are going on at one time to gain perspective or focus.

In Winners, they harmonize with each other into three concentric zones of growth, each complementing the others—together making up "The Winners' Circle of Life."

The Outer Circle, your outside world, contains the many outside influences which act upon you and upon which you act. It is the arena outside of yourself, where your professional, social, family, educational, and leisure activities take place. Tremendous abundance everywhere!

How many sunrises and sunsets have you watched this month? How many good books have you read and how many informative audio cassette programs have you listened to this month? When was your last trip to Australia to watch the Koala climb the eucalyptus tree? Is your education continuing? How's your sailboat? How's your family? Have you fed or clothed an orphan this month? How's your income relative to inflation? Are you secure or looking forward to Social Security? Are you giving and getting enough in your Outer Circle—your environmental world?

The next related circle in your life houses your physiological self—all the skin, bones, cells, parts, and muscles that make up your physical being. More abundance! (In many of us, too much abundance from overeating!)

How's your body these days? Are you fat and sluggish? Are you gaunt and nervous? Do you puff going up a flight of stairs? What kind of fuel do you put in your magnificent

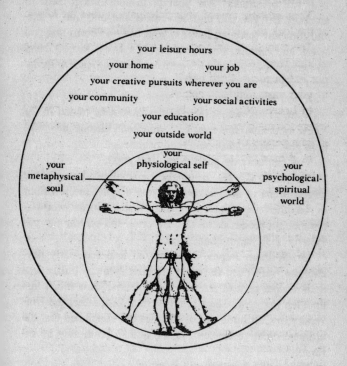

machine, your one and only transportation vehicle for life? Is it full of smoke? Are your brain and liver pickled in alcohol? Do you use high-test meals and nutrition or hit-and-run, low-test junk food? Is your body a Ferrari that you tweak and tune for the Grand Prix? Or is it a rackety heap parked by the curb to get you from birth to death with the least number of overhauls?

If you abuse it, you won't get to use it as long.

Winners know that their bodies cannot be traded in for a new model and that their performance in the outside world is largely dependent upon good health.

You can only do good if you feel good.

The Inner Circle, seemingly the smallest, is really the largest arena of all and controls your actions and reactions in the other two arenas. It is your mental/spiritual world— the thought processes inside your brain and central nervous system. Talk about abundance!

Dr. William James, a recognized leader in early psychology, said even the most effective humans utilize less than ten per cent of their mental potential. It is much *less* than ten per cent. The Brain Research Institute at the University of California at Los Angeles has concluded that the ultimate creative capacity of the human brain may be infinite.

No limits other than self-imposed!

Your brain is a Xerox machine, a Polaroid camera, a Betamax video tape recorder, a Technicolor widescreen projector, a thousand IBM computers, plus ten billion miniature microfilm cartridges all delicately designed into one storage battery, floating in an electrochemical solution.

With this virtually untapped and limitless resource, why aren't we more creative, inventive and successful?

Laziness, to be sure, is one mental block. Why bother?

Fear is another big block. "It's too risky for me!"

And a low self-image, resulting from negative attitudes,

is the major "energy gap" preventing the release of full human actualization.

Attitude is the answer. In order to feel good physically and do good in the outer world, you need to get your head together with constructive thinking—not superficial lip service, but dedicated learning of new, healthy responses to the stimuli of life.

There are ten attitudinal qualities in the ten chapters that follow, that seem to be found in winning human beings without regard to sex, color, creed, or circumstance. These ten common denominators of healthy, winning behavior that transform average, common people into high performance, uncommon achievers are old friends of yours. You have read about them, talked about them and experimented with them all throughout your life.

I offer these Ten Qualities of the Total Winner to you as a "winning combination" to play your own ball game with—however lofty or humble your goals.

Put yourself together. Play it as you see it. But play to Win!

It's no scrimmage or practice game. It's your Superbowl every day!

TEN QUALITIES
OF A TOTAL WINNER

"Oh wad some power the giftie
   gie us
To see oursels as others see us
It wad frae monie a blunder
   free us
   An foolish notion."
                    —Robert Burns

CHAPTER **1** —————————————————————

POSITIVE SELF-AWARENESS

Antonyms:
Dishonesty, insensitivity, "tunnel vision"

Synonyms:
Self-honesty, empathy, open-ness

Losers' Self-talk:
"The world is flat and that is that."

Winners' Self-talk:
"I understand where I am coming from."

Proverb:
"O Great Spirit, grant me the wisdom to walk in another Indian's moccasins."

Winners are more aware. They display a *Positive Self-awareness*. They are well aware of how little they really know about anything in their world, and that what they do know is shaded by their own heredity and environment.

Winners are eager to learn—especially about their own potential contribution to the quality of life. They are keenly aware of the abundance available to them.

Winners are honest. Not just with other people's money or confidences. They are honest with themselves.

Positive Self-awareness is self-honesty. Winners are honest about their potential and honest about the time and effort necessary for top achievement.

Winners can look in the mirror and see what lies behind their own eyes. You are a Winner when what you think, how you feel, and what you do—are nearly consistent.

Losers are unaware of what is happening (or lie about it) in their environments, unaware of the needs of others, and unaware of their own personal involvement with life.

Winners are sensitive. They are more tuned-in and more turned-on than others around. They don't need drugs or external stimulants to make life "a happening."

They are turned-on naturally.

Losers become hardened, cold and closed to new ideas and new opportunities. This hardness can range from intellectual cynicism, to indifference and apathy, to prejudice and aloofness, to vulgarity and rudeness.

Losers suffer from hardening of the arteries connecting their insights with their hindsights and foresights.

Losers are narrow-minded human beings.

Winners are open. They see the many alternatives in every situation. They look at "relative" rather than "absolute" facts.

Positive Self-awareness is open-mindedness.

Are you open-minded?

Do you look at life through your parents' eyeglasses? Are your prejudices inherited, or are they your own?

Is your skin white and so you wish you could sport a deep bronze tan all year-round? Or is your skin brown or black and do you wish maybe it was white? Is black beautiful, and white . . . sickly and pale? Is white rich and black poor? Or is black gold and white trash?

Positive Self-awareness is realizing that each human being on earth is a person with equal rights to fulfill his or her own potential in life.

Positive Self-awareness is realizing that skin color, birthplace, religious beliefs, sex, financial status, and intelligence are not measures of worth or worthiness.

Positive Self-awareness is accepting the fact that every human being is a distinctly unique individual—and thinking how good that is! No two people are alike, not even identical twins.

We are unique in our fingerprints. Unique in our footprints, even in our lip-prints! Bell Telephone has discovered that each of us speaks with a sound frequency unmatched by any other person and is in the process of developing a "Voice-print" system that will provide instant, positive identification electronically. Before the year 2000, it will be possible to do away with ID cards, credit cards, phone calls to banks, signature comparisons, and fingerprint checks. By stating your name audibly into a microphone at the counter, window or check-stand, your "Voice-print" frequency will be compared with the one on file at a central computer. No more phony checks or stolen credit cards!

We speak at different frequencies and think at different frequencies. How many times have you heard people say: "We're not on the same wavelength!" We, in the human race, have been trying to get on the same wavelength for many centuries.

The pursuit of mind-expanding techniques toward a heightened state of awareness has been a mysterious journey beginning, perhaps, in the high mountains of Tibet. Today, the quest for mental and physical self-awareness ranges from the ridiculous to the sublime—from electronic hi-fi, stereo Alpha brain wave simulators, to hashish, to LSD trips, to est, to horoscopes, to Moonies, to biorhythms, to the quiet meditation of Maharishi Mahesh Yogi.

No wonder there is so much discord in family, social and international life. Everyone hears a different drummer, sees through a different lens, perceives through a different filter, and decides as a result of a different computer program in his or her own unique brain.

The ability to accept the fact that everyone is unique and to be able to understand another person's point of view, as if you were that person, is the definition of "Empathy."

Empathy is the ability to walk in another Indian's moccasins for a mile before passing judgment.

Empathy is "feeling with" someone else. Sympathy is "feeling for" someone else.

Empathy is when you watch the marathon runners at the 20-mile mark—and your own legs ache.

Empathy is watching a re-run of the movie "Rocky" and hardly being able to lift your arms at the end of round 15.

Empathy is crawling into another person's being and looking at yourself through his or her eyes.

Ask yourself the questions:

How would I like to have a husband like me if I were my wife?

How would I like to have a mother like me if I were my children?

How would I like to have a manager like me if I were my employee?

What would it feel like to be a white shoeshine boy in downtown Nairobi?

How would it feel to be an illegal American alien in Mexico City?

How does the world appear through the eyes of a child?

The best example of newly-found empathy I can recall, is told by James Newman as it related to a student in one of his highly-regarded PACE seminars for couples:

"A lady took her five-year-old son shopping at the Broadway during the Christmas season. She knew he would enjoy all the decorations, window dressings, carol music, toys, and Santa Claus.

"Soon after they arrived, however, the boy began to cry softly and cling to his mother's coat.

"'Good grief, what are you fussing about?' she scolded. 'Santa doesn't visit cry babies!'

"'Oh well, maybe it's because your shoe's untied.' She knelt down in the aisle beside him to tie his shoe . . . and as she knelt, she happened to look up.

"For the first time, she viewed her world through the eyes of a five-year-old!

"No baubles, bangles, presents, or gaily decorated table displays—just a maze of aisles too high to see over . . . giant legs, fannies and feet pushing and shoving, bumping and thumping! Rather than fun, it looked terrifying!

"She took her child right home and vowed never to impose her version of fun on him again. She had had a rare experience of empathy with a five-year-old that too few of us grown-ups ever share."

Here's a little poem that may help you remember to practice empathy with your own children:

"TAKE A MOMENT TO HEAR TODAY,
WHAT YOUR CHILDREN HAVE TO SAY
LISTEN TODAY . . . WHATEVER YOU DO
OR THEY WON'T BE THERE . . .
TO LISTEN TO YOU!"

The same goes for empathy with teenagers, young adults, foreigners, and others whom you view as "different" from yourself.

Does it exasperate you to discover that there are so many weird people around compared to you? Did it ever occur to you that you may seem really weird to others, too? What is weird for certain?

What is certain is that we need to understand what being human is . . . and that is a changing, growing, imperfect, but amazing living creation.

Winners have that marvelous ability to understand their own relationship to their environments and to the many people and events that interact in everyday life.

Winners realize that "adaptability" is the key to success, to mental and physical health, and even the key to survival in today's world full of sensory bombardment.

During the past fifty years, electronic advances in telephone, television, satellite, and computerized communications have accelerated to the point where we are subjected to more information transactions in a single day, than our grandparents experienced in their entire lifetimes . . . *more in one of our days today than in all of their lives*.

In our evolution during the past 500,000 years, there has been little change, if any, in our ability to cope with or adapt to our rapidly changing society.

And here is an important key to Winning Self-awareness: Winners learn how to relax and cope with the trials and tribulations of everyday life, without popping "uppers" when they are depressed, and Valium when they are anxious.

Winners develop mental toughness, which we commonly

refer to as strength of character. Experiments have proven that adversities and failures in our lives, if adapted to and viewed as normal corrective feedback to use to get back on target, serve to develop in us an immunity against anxiety, depression and the adverse responses to stress.

The anti-anxiety drugs, in increasing use in the United States today (over 60 million tablets consumed annually), serve to reduce emotional reactions to the threat of pain or failure: that is why they are taken. But unfortunately, they also interfere with the ability to learn to tolerate these stresses. It is far better to develop behavioral methods of coping with one's problems than to dissolve them with a pill.

Winners know that little has changed since the days of their early ancestors when—at the first hint of a dangerous or threatening confrontation—the body automatically mustered its defenses in preparation for Fight or Flight. Instead of a sabre-tooth-tiger-a-week or a dinosaur-a-month... today it is at least one or two unwelcome or unpleasant interpersonal surprises before bedtime rolls around each night. How many complete strangers, whom you'll never meet in person, got you uptight and ready to risk your life on the freeway today?

Losers in life over-react to what is happening like cave dwellers. They flare to anger quickly and get defensive easily. Their blood pressure jumps, as their heart rate quickens, as their arteries constrict, as the adrenalin pumps... as they rush headlong into an imaginary struggle for survival, or as they run and hide from imaginary predators and volcanic eruptions.

The effects of this type of daily "distress" or negative stress are devastating to the mental and physical health of the individual. As a result, the Loser drinks more, smokes more, frets more, and pops more pills to cope or escape.

Dr. Robert Eliot, member of the Board of Governors of the American College of Cardiology and President of the International Stress Foundation, is studying the relationship between stress and heart attacks, strokes and other diseases of today. Dr. Eliot refers to the syndrome of "invisible entrapment" or the deep-seated worries, frustrations and anxieties of people unable to cope effectively with their changing status in a changing world, as major factors in the increasing incidence of sudden death from heart attacks and other mental and physical illnesses.

While we are in the process of winning the battle against infectious diseases attacking us from outside ourselves, we seem to be losing ground to those that result from our own inner conflicts.

Positive Self-awareness is one important part of ultimate victory. Dr. Hans Selye in Montreal, acknowledged world pioneer of early stress research, has suggested in his books and in several face-to-face interviews with me, that each individual should try to find his or her own healthy stress level in life and operate within that level. He generally categorizes us as "racehorses" or "turtles" by nature—and everyone knows that a racehorse loves to run and will die if it is corralled and confined . . . while a turtle will die from exhaustion if forced to run on a treadmill, moving too fast for his own, unique, step-by-step nature.

While expressing emotions such as love, joy, compassion, and exhilaration is healthy and desirable . . . it may be beneficial to us if we can minimize the overt expression of hostility, anger, depression, loneliness, and anxiety. The only healthy expression of the Fight or Flight emotion is in the face of a life or death situation. In most of our daily confrontations, hostility and anger can be dealt with by deep breathing, relaxation and an exercise program involving gross physical impact such as running, racquetball, handball, or tennis. If we want to conquer undesirable emotional tendencies in ourselves, we must learn to go through the "outward movements" of the desirable, positive dispositions that we prefer to cultivate.

One of the wisest physicians, Sir William Osler, stated

to his medical students: "Imperturbability is the essential bodily virtue. It is coolness and presence of mind under all circumstances . . . calmness amid storm . . . clearness of judgment in moments of grave peril." Adaptability is the key. By anticipating the probable action of others through empathy and by remaining open and flexible, we will not allow others to ruin our days with their bad days, to rain on our parades.

One of the best ways to develop adaptability to the stresses of life is to view them as normal. Earl Nightingale tells of his visit with his son recently to the Great Barrier Reef which stretches nearly 1800 miles from New Guinea to Australia. Noticing that the coral polyps on the inside of the reef, where the sea was tranquil and quiet in the lagoon, appeared pale and lifeless . . . while the coral on the outside of the reef, subject to the surge of the tide and power of the waves, were bright and vibrant with splendid colors and flowing growth . . . Earl Nightingale asked his guide why this was so.

"It's very simple," came the reply, "the coral on the lagoon-side dies rapidly with no challenge for growth and survival . . . while the coral facing the surge and power of the open sea, thrives and multiplies because it is challenged and tested every day. And so it is with every living organism on earth."

Positive Self-awareness is realizing that a person who does not read is no better than the person who cannot read— and that the person who does not continue to learn, to adapt and grow, is no better than one who cannot grow.

Positive Self-awareness is that "moment of truth" which every Winner experiences as the first and most important step in self-development: It is understanding how much potential and abundance we have, and how little we have done to challenge our minds.

It is understanding that we must seek and walk with truth every day of our lives and always be open to different alternatives and better ways to win. The foundation upon which every great life has been built includes the three cornerstones of truth, integrity and honesty. They must be present for any real and lasting success of any kind. All we really need to learn, accept and internalize to be a healthy human being with Positive Self-awareness under every circumstance, is to ask ourselves, "Is this true?" "Is this honest?" If we can answer, "Yes," or if we can seek the truth from someone who has experienced it, we can move ahead to action with the solid realization that we have taken care of the Cause, and that the Effect will take care of itself.

Winners, with this awareness, are sensitive to the needs and differences of others... aware that the clock is always running... knowing that there is still time to Win.

But no time to Lose.

REVIEW

(Read this Positive Self-awareness Review several times over the period of one month to etch it in your memory.)

Winners know who they are, what they believe, the role in life they are presently filling, their great personal potential—and the future roles and goals which will mark fulfillment of that potential. They have learned these things, and are constantly adding to their knowledge, through experience, insight, feedback, and judgment. As a result they can continuously not only "play from strength" in the game of life, but also avoid errors and correct weaknesses. Their judgments are characterized by extreme honesty. They don't kid others and they don't kid themselves. Losers say, "Who knows what I could do if I only had a chance." Winners say, "I know who I am, where I'm coming from and where I'm going."

Make this moment the moment of truth about yourself. You have been selling yourself short all of your life. You have the opportunity to experience more environmental, physical and mental/spiritual abundance than you could use in ten lifetimes. Open up your lenses to the possibilities and alternatives available in your life. Change your attitude and your lifestyle and your many environments will change automatically. Understand your own uniqueness. Appreciate the differences in others. Relax and learn to respond positively to stress. Change for the better that which can be changed. Remove from your presence those negative influences that cannot be changed. Adapt and adjust to those negative influences that cannot be changed or removed.

Take Action Today for More Positive Self-awareness:

1. *Schedule a comprehensive annual physical* with your own physician or a reputable clinic. Not just a blood pressure, urine test and thank you exam. Every two years, schedule yourself at a Mayo or Scripps Clinic, or with your physician, for an even more detailed physical. Get the works—blood work, EKG, upper and lower G.I. series x-rays, eyes, etc. Don't wait for the flat tire, engine knock, or dead battery. Get a prevention check and a tune-up. Make that appointment for a teeth cleaning session you have been putting off and start using the dental floss that's been sitting in your medicine cabinet. Call now or in the morning for that physical exam. Don't put it off—do it!

2. *Be more curious about everything* in your world. Read book digests, so that you can share all of the best sellers. Listen to audio cassettes. Take your librarian to lunch! Go to seminars and lectures concerning the healthy mind and body. Seek out and gain counsel from the most successful people in your profession and hobbies. (They love to talk about their experiences and are surprisingly eager to help others.)

3. *Break the daily and weekly routine* you have set. Get out of that comfortable rut. Unplug the TV for a month. Go to work via a different route or by another mode of transportation. Take the kids to a symphony or puppet show. Plan a skiing trip to Chile on the Fourth of July. Have your children give one of their best toys to an orphan this Christmas. If you take showers, take a bath for a change. Instead of taking a Valium, take a walk near flowers and trees!

4. *Make a list of "I Am's"*—Two columns. Assets or "I Am Good At" in one column. Liabilities or "I Need Improvement In" in the other column. Pick your ten best traits and your ten traits needing most improvement. Take the first three liabilities and schedule an activity or find a winner who will help you improve in each of the three areas. Forget about the rest of the liabilities. Remember, relish and dwell on all ten of your best assets. They'll take you anywhere you want to go in life!

5. *Look at yourself through other people's eyes.* Imagine being your parents. Imagine being that person married to you. Imagine being your child. When you walk into a room or office, imagine that each person is thinking two descriptive adjectives about you—such as "well-dressed, confident" or "aloof, nervous." What would they be in each case about you? Why?

6. *Look at yourself through your own eyes objectively.* This is easier said than done for all of us. If you want to test this exercise, try standing in front of a full-length mirror with no clothes on, with only a grocery bag over your head, with eye holes cut out. Look at yourself from front, rear and side views. Talk about a mind-blowing experience! When you look in the mirror day after day—your friendly face is used to seeing yourself and has rationalized all of your flaws—even the flab and dark circles. With the paper sack over that well-known face, you become a stranger in the nude. It's an experience you will remember for weeks to come.

7. *Take 30 precious minutes each day for you alone.* Relax and breathe deeply from the pelvis and stomach up into your lungs when you inhale. Exhale slowly. Meditate and let go as if you were lying in the center of a water bed the size of a football field. Float freely. Give yourself at least one beautiful half-hour out of every twenty-four to be completely

aware that your life belongs to you and that all that exists in your life is seen out of your eyes and experienced by your mind and body.

8. *Look for truth and speak the truth*. Don't let the ads and the fads make you one of the countless victims of greed. When you read something that impresses you, check the source. When in doubt, call the research department of a national publication you trust or call a major university you respect. If it really works wonders, it will be available everywhere like aspirin. If it's a breakthrough, look for it to be announced by reputable news authorities and government agencies. Rather than hearing what you want to hear, listen for the facts of the matter. And remember, everything you think is your opinion, based upon your impressions from limited sources. Keep expanding your sources from the best authorities. View everything with a certain open-minded skepticism . . . open-minded enough to explore it without prejudice . . . and skeptical enough to research and test its validity.

9. *Be aware of the children and the elderly*. Remember that childhood is that wonderful, special classroom in which the adult is developed. Listen to their dreams. Observe their special talents. Ask for their opinions and reactions. Also, remember that becoming elderly is inevitable. It can be a lonely or glorious time. With activities, goals, horizons, and attention, being a senior citizen can be as exciting as being a senior in high school. It's a question of Positive Self-awareness.

10. *Be empathic*. Learn to feel how others feel and consider where they are coming from before criticizing or passing judgment. Even if you can't feel *for* everyone you meet, be certain that you feel *with* every living thing you encounter. It's the key to Positive Self-awareness.

Love yourself
Then give away
All the love
You feel
Today.

CHAPTER 2

POSITIVE SELF-ESTEEM

Antonyms:
Self-deprecation, self-doubt, self-consciousness

Synonyms:
Self-worth, self-respect, self-confidence

Losers' Self-talk:
"I'd rather be someone else."

Winners' Self-talk:
"I like myself."

Proverb:
"If you love yourself, then you can give love.
How can you give what you don't have?"

Positive Self-esteem is one of the most important and basic qualities of a winning human being. It is that deep down, inside the self, feeling of your own worth.

"You know, I like myself. I really do like myself. Given my parents and my background, I'm glad I'm me. I'd rather be me than anyone else, living at any other time in history."

This is the self-talk of a Winner... and positive self-talk is the key to developing Positive Self-esteem.

Winners have developed strong beliefs of self-worth and self-confidence. They weren't necessarily born with these good feelings, but as with every other habit, they have learned to like themselves through practice.

Some individuals are born with much more going for them at the start:

Wealthy parents, beautiful parents, talented and intelligent parents. And many children, in their early years, have been encouraged and nurtured by winning parents, outstanding teachers, coaches and friends who gave them early feelings of self-esteem. And this is perhaps the most important quality of a good parent... and also a good business leader... the positive encouragment of their children—and employees—toward the development of self-worth.

But there is an amazing historical pattern that's almost contradictory, and that is the pattern that some of the offspring of the richest, most beautiful, most prominent and talented people... have become Losers... unable to live up to their heritage and unable to accept themselves or perform effectively in society on their own. This may be because they had so much going for them at the start that they developed no inner drive to take them forward. And yet, some chidren from the most backward, discouraging beginnings . . . have grown into outstanding Winners and top achievers in every walk of life. Out of adversity can come greatness.

When we examine Losers and low-achievers, an attitude of low self-esteem seems to be at the root of their problems. Recent studies of aircraft skyjackers and assassins of world leaders have shown that these aggressors are very likely to be loners with extremely low self-esteem. The same is true with most criminals.

To develop an even higher degree of Positive Self-esteem, Winners learn to understand that self-development is a lifetime program. As we were growing up, many of us played an inferior role to the adults in our lives. We were told what to do and what not to do. We were constantly reminded of our shortcomings in phrases such as, "Don't interrupt, children should be seen and not heard!" "Don't touch, you're not old enough to do that!" "Here, let Dad show you how to do it right!"

This bombardment can take its toll, and if practiced continually, can create the troubled teens and the generation gap. Low achievers water and cultivate the early seeds of inferior feelings with their imaginations and develop a strong, prickly weed which sticks and irritates for years to come.

Scientists have been studying a native tribe in South America members of which have been dying prematurely of a strange malady for many generations. It was finally discovered that the disease was caused by the bite of an insect which lives in the walls of their adobe homes. The natives have several possible solutions . . . they can destroy the insects with an insecticide; they can destroy and rebuild

their homes; they can move to another area where there are
no such insects; or they can continue to live and die early,
just as they have done for generations. They have chosen
to remain as they are and die early, the path of least resistance and no change.

Many people have a similar attitude about personal development. On the one hand, they know that learning brings
about change, but on the other hand, they resist change.
They know that many people have overcome enormous obstacles to become great, but they can't imagine it happening
to them. And so they resign themselves to be the also-rans
in life, wishing and envying away their lives. These low-
achievers learn the habit of concentrating on their failures
and the negative events in their lives with self-talk that
reinforces the losing cycle. Because they are controlled by
external standards set by others, they often set their sights
too high and are unrealistic to begin with and as they fail
to reach their goals again and again, these failures become
set in their subconscious self-images as targets and goals of
their own. This explains why so many people have permanent potential. In other words, why they *almost* succeed
over and over, having temporary, fleeting successes, which
fail to materialize into a solid lifestyle.

It's also interesting to note that the blowhards in life, the
ones who yell loudest for service and attention, are really
calling for help because of low self-esteem. What they are
really shouting is "Help, look at me, please!" It is said that
John Dillinger ran into a farmhouse and repeatedly told the
occupants, "My name is John Dillinger. I'm not going to
hurt you—I just wanted you to know that my name is
Dillinger."

Psychiatrist Bernard Holland has pointed out that although juvenile delinquents appear to be very independent
and have a reputation of being braggarts, particularly about
how they hate everyone in authority, they protest too much.
Underneath this hard exterior shell, says Dr. Holland, "is

a soft vulnerable inner person who wants to be dependent upon others." However, they cannot get close to anyone because they will not trust anyone. At some time in the past they were hurt by a person important to them, and they dare not leave themselves open to be hurt again. They must always have their defenses up. To prevent further rejection and pain, they attack first. Thus they drive away the very people who would love them, if given half a chance, and could help them. This description also applies to many people we associate with who are not juvenile delinquents. They may be professional peers or even loved ones.

Many people we know are hurt terribly by little things we call "social slights." It is a well-known psychological fact that the people who become offended the easiest have the lowest self-esteem. It is the person who feels undeserving, doubts his own capabilities, and has a poor opinion of himself who becomes jealous at the drop of a hat. Jealousy, which is the scourge of many marriages, is nearly always caused by self-doubt. The person with adequate self-esteem doesn't feel hostile toward others, isn't out to prove anything, can see the facts more clearly, and isn't demanding in his claims on other people.

There is a growing tendency today among many individuals to display an array of expensive possessions and outward trappings of affluence. This concentration on status symbols is more likely to say to others that the owner is lacking in self-esteem, rather than that he is rich. It is possible that only those with a strong sense of self-worth can afford to display a modest image to the community.

The word "esteem" literally means to appreciate the value of. Why do we stand in awe of the power and immensity of the sea, the uniqueness of a solar eclipse, the beauty of a flower, a giant redwood, or a sunset, and at the same time, downgrade ourselves? Didn't the same Creator make us? Are we not the most marvelous creation of all, able to think, experience, change our environment, and love? Don't downgrade the product just because you haven't used it properly and effectively.

Confidence is built upon the experience of success. When we begin anything new we usually have little confidence because we have not learned from experience that we can succeed. This is true with learning to ride a bicycle, skiing, figure skating, flying a high performance jet aircraft, and leading people. It is true that success breeds success. Winners focus on past successes and forget past failures. They use errors and mistakes as a way to learning—then they dismiss them from their minds.

Yet, what do many of us do? We destroy our self-confidence by remembering past failures and forgetting all about our past successes. We not only remember failures, we etch them in our minds with emotion. We condemn ourselves. Winners know that it doesn't matter how many times they have failed in the past. What matters is their successes which should be remembered, reinforced and dwelt upon.

To establish true self-esteem, we must concentrate on our successes and look at the failures and negatives in our lives only as corrective feedback to get us on target again. The child's view must be recognized as just that; as serving a purpose in early years, but dropping aside as we mature. Instead of comparing ourselves to others, we should view ourselves in terms of our own abilities, interests and goals. We can begin by making a conscious effort to upgrade our lifestyle and pay more attention to personal appearance and personal habits.

To develop more Positive Self-esteem we need to base more of our actions and decisions on rational thinking rather than on emotions. Emotions are automatic subconscious reactions. To respond to the daily experiences and challenges of life by reacting emotionally is to nullify the wisdom and power of the rational mind. Winners are able to enjoy their emotions—like children probing the depths of love, excitement, joy, and compassion; but they make the decisions that shape their lives through logic and common sense. Marriages today would be much stronger if they were entered into intelligently, as well as emotionally.

To develop and maintain the self-esteem we need to find pleasure and pride in our current profession rather than looking for greener pastures elsewhere. This is the philosophy of mining your "Acres of Diamonds" right now, right where you are—making changes in your internal reactions rather than searching for external stimulation in a new environment.

Although we are always seeking improvement, the Winner with Positive Self-esteem can accept himself or herself just as he or she is at this moment. Since the perfect human has not been discovered, we all need to live with our hangups and idiosyncracies... until they can be ironed out. One of the most important aspects of self-esteem that accounts for successful, dynamic living is that of self-acceptance— the willingness to be oneself and live one's life as it is unfolding, accepting all responsibility for the ultimate outcome. Shakespeare explained it when, in *Hamlet*, he had Polonius say: "And this above all, to thine own self be true—and it must follow as the night the day—thou can'st not then be false, to any man."

Perhaps the most important key to the permanent enhancement of self-esteem is the practice of positive self-talk. Every waking moment we must feed our subconscious self-images positive thoughts about ourselves and our performances... so relentlessly and vividly that our self-images are in time modified to conform to the new, higher standards.

Current research on the effect of words and images on the functions of the body offers amazing evidence of the power that words, spoken at random, can have on body functions monitored on biofeedback equipment. Since thoughts can raise and lower body temperature, secrete hormones, relax muscles and nerve endings, dilate and constrict

arteries, and raise and lower pulse rate—it is obvious that
we need to control the language we use on ourselves. That's
why Winners rarely "put themselves down" in actions or in
words. Losers fall into the trap of saying: "I can't"... "I'm
a klutz"... "I wish"... "Yeah, but"... "I shoulda" and...
"I mighta."

Winners use constructive feedback and self-talk every
day: "I can"... "I look forward"... "Next time, I'll get it
right"... "I'm feeling better."

One good indicator of an individual's opinion of himself
is the way he can accept a compliment. It is incredible how
low-achievers belittle and demean themselves when others
try to pay them value:

"I'd like to congratulate you on a job well done."

"Oh, it was nothing... I was just lucky I guess."

"Wow, that was a great shot you made!"

"Yeah, I had my eyes closed."

"That's a good looking suit, is it new?"

"No, I've been thinking of giving it to the Goodwill."

The Loser believes that the quality of humility should be
pushed over the cliff into humorous humiliation. And the
devasting fact is that the robot self-image is always listening
and accepts these negative barbs as facts to store as reality.

The Winners in life accept compliments by simply saying
"thank you." Bob Hope says "thank you"; Frank Boorman
says "thank you"; Steve Cauthen, after winning the Triple
Crown, doesn't say "Gee, I almost fell off my horse"; he
says, "thank you." Neil Armstrong, Jack Nicklaus, Tom
Watson, Cheryl Tiegs, Nancy Lopez, Chris Evert all say
"thank you." Self-esteem is the quality of simply saying
"thank you," and accepting value that is paid to you by
others.

In the studies of Winners who have pulled themselves
up and who remain at the top in life, a high self-esteem
seems to be the common denominator. Benjamin Franklin,
Thomas Edison, Jonas Salk, Golda Meir—have all written

about early feelings of self-worth. And look at Helen Keller, who though blind and deaf, dedicated her life to helping the less fortunate . . . and Albert Einstein, who failed his college entrance exams . . . and Galileo, who was groomed to be a tailor, but dropped out of the factory into history . . . and Abe Lincoln, who failed at what he tried to do so many times that he should have given up . . . and Menachem Begin of Israel, who began as a street urchin in a Polish ghetto . . . and the desert peasant boy, who was falsely imprisoned for treason as a young officer in Egypt's wastelands and yet went on to become its president . . . Anwar Sadat.

Almost without exception, the real Winner, whether we speak of sports, business, or any other activity of life, has accepted his own uniqueness, feels comfortable with his image, and is willing that others know and accept him just as he is. And, it is an interesting fact that such a person naturally attracts friends and supporters. He or she seldom has to stand alone.

Bernard Baruch was once asked how he went about arranging the seating of guests for his dinner parties without offending anybody. He replied that he solved the problem by simply allowing his guests to seat themselves, choosing where they wished to sit. As he put it, "The people who matter don't mind, and the people who mind . . . don't matter." The principle that Baruch uncovered is true in all walks of life. Those who know who they are need not be defensive—nor do they have to go out of their way to improve anything. Their solid self-esteem is quite enough to get them anywhere they want to go.

Winners are aware of their potential. They like who they are. Since they have a deep feeling of their own worth, they are eager to love others as they do themselves. Positive Self-esteem . . . one of the most important qualities of a Winner. Talk yourself up!

There is no time to Lose.

REVIEW

(Read this Positive Self-esteem Review several times over the period of one month to etch it in your memory.)

Winners have a deep-down feeling of their own worth. They know that, contrary to popular belief, this feeling of self-acceptance and deserving is not necessarily a legacy from wise and loving parents—history is full of saints who rose from the gutters and literal monsters who grew up in loving families. Winners are not outer-directed. Recognizing their uniqueness they develop and maintain their own high standards. Though they recognize the universality of fear and anxiety, Winners don't give in to these emotions. Losing self-talk: "I'd rather be somebody else." Winning self-talk: "I do things well because I'm that kind of a person."

Accept yourself as you are right now—an imperfect, changing, growing and worthwhile person. Realize that liking yourself and feeling that you're a super individual in your own special way is not necessarily egotistical. In addition to taking pride in what you are accomplishing—and even more importantly—enjoy the unique person that you are just in being alive right now. Understand the truth that although we as individuals are not born with equal physical and mental attributes, we are born with equal rights to feel the excitement and joy in believing that we deserve the very best in life. Most successful people believe in their own worth, even when they have nothing but a dream to hold on to. Perhaps more than any other quality, healthy self-esteem is the door to high achievement and happiness.

Take Action Today for
More Positive Self-esteem:

1. *Dress and look your best at all times* regardless of the pressure from your friends and peers. Personal grooming and lifestyle appearance provide an instantaneous projection on the surface of how you feel inside about yourself.

2. *Volunteer your own name first* in every telephone call and whenever you meet someone new. By paying value to your own name in communication, you are developing the habit of paying value to yourself as an individual.

3. *Take inventory of your good reasons for self-esteem today.* Write down what your "BAG" is. Blessings—who and what you are thankful for. Accomplishments—what you have done that you're proud of so far. Goals—what your dreams and ambitions are.

4. *Respond with a simple, courteous "thank you"* when anyone pays you a compliment for any reason.

5. *Sit up front in the most prominent rows* when you attend meetings, lectures and conferences. Your purpose for going is to listen, learn and possibly exchange questions and answers with the key speakers.

6. *Walk more erectly and authoritatively in public* with a relaxed but more rapid pace. It has been proven that individuals who walk erectly and briskly usually are confident about themselves and where they are going.

7. *Set your own internal standards* rather than comparing yourself to others. Keep upgrading your own standards in

lifestyle, behavior, professional accomplishment, relationships, etc.

8. *Use encouraging, affirmative language* when you talk to yourself and to others about yourself. Focus on uplifting and building adjectives and adverbs. Everything you say about yourself is subconsciously being recorded by others and, more importantly, by your own self-image.

9. *Keep a self-development plan ongoing at all times.* Sketch it out on paper—the knowledge you'll require, the behavior modification you'll achieve, the changes in your life that will result. Seek out the real winners in life as friends and role models. Misery loves company, but so does success!

10. *SMILE!* In every language, in every culture—it is the light in your window that tells people there's a caring, sharing individual inside and it's the universal code for "I'm O.K.—You're O.K., too!"

Losers live in classic style
In the never land called
  "Someday I'll"
Winners live each day as if their
  last
Not in the future, nor in the past
And someday . . . becomes now!

CHAPTER 3

POSITIVE SELF-CONTROL

Antonyms:
Irresponsibility, indecision, chance

Synonyms:
Self-determination, volition, choice

Losers' Self-talk:
"It always happens to me."

Winners' Self-talk:
"I make it happen for me."

Proverb:
"Life is a do-it-myself project. I take the credit or the blame for my performance."

Winners "make" it happen. Losers "let" it happen.

The true meaning of self-control is often misunderstood. Many people interpret self-control as "getting a good grip on yourself" or remaining cool and passive under pressure.

Self-control, as it relates to the Psychology of Winning, is synonymous with self-determination.

Winners take full responsibility for determining their actions in their own lives. They believe in Cause and Effect, and have the philosophy that life is a "do-it-to-yourself" program.

Self-control implies freedom for individuals to choose among many alternatives and to shape their own destinies.

Many people believe that "Fate," luck, or possibly their astrological sign have shaped the outcome of their lives. These people who feel that life is mostly determined by circumstances, predestination or being at the right place at the right time, are more likely to give in to doubt and fear.

People who are aware that they exert control over what happens to them in life are happier and are able to choose more appropriate responses to whatever occurs.

Those who cannot make up their minds for fear of making the wrong choice, vacillating in indecision, simply do not achieve their goals—a requisite for success. Rather, they take their place among the rank and file of the also-rans, trudging along in bland mediocrity.

50

All individuals are what they are—and where they are—as a composite result of all their own doings. It is true that we are all God-created—but we all also are "self-molded." Although our innate characteristics and environments are given to us initially, the decisions we make determine whether we win or lose our particular game of life.

Voltaire likened life to a game of cards. Each player must accept the cards life deals him or her. But once they are in hand, he or she alone must decide how to play the cards in order to win the game.

The writer, John Erskine, put it a little differently when he wrote: "Though we sometimes speak of a primrose path, we all know that a bad life is just as difficult, just as full of work, obstacles and hardships, as a good one. The only choice is the kind of life one would care to spend one's efforts on."

Whether you are a bum on skid row or a happy individual—you can pat yourself on the back, taking the credit or the blame for your place in life. You took over control from your parents when you were very young and have been in the driver's seat ever since.

I didn't realize until I was thirty-five that I'm behind the wheel in my life. I thought it was the government, inflation and my heritage. I used to think that as a Gemini, I was destined to be creative, but non-specific.

I should have taken a hint from one of my daughters when she was only eleven months old. She was in her highchair for dinner, and I decided she should eat some nourishing, strained squash.

I tasted it to test the temperature. (It wasn't delicious, but I knew it was good for her.) I held the little curved spoonful out and gently entreated, "Open up, Honey, Daddy has some yummy squash for you."

She stared coldly at me and clamped her mouth shut in passive defiance.

Being in total control of the situation, I simply pressed her cheeks firmly with two fingers, thus forcing her mouth open. I then neatly inserted the spoonful of squash in her mouth and quietly (but sternly) ordered, "Go on . . . swallow it . . . it's good for you."

She spit it out onto the tray and all over my necktie! She had decided at age eleven months that she didn't like strained squash!

And so children do begin to take control of their lives at an early age. Many chidren learn how to control their parents' lives as well, long before they know how to talk in complete sentences.

Whining receives attention. Crying receives consolation. Begging begets goodies. Tantrums create havoc. It is easy to incite Mommy against Daddy and sit back and watch the show. Just like on TV!

There's a disturbing trend among young parents all over the United States today to be at the mercy of their babies and little tots. It is especially noticeable on cross-country trips aboard commercial airliners where the parents are not able to exert enough control to even keep seat belts on their kids long enough for take-off and landing. The same trend is spreading throughout the school system in this country from nursery school through high school.

I know one couple, both graduates of one of our major universities, who have so little control that—in order to get their five-year-old to bed while I was visiting—they had to put cookies on the stairs so he would eat himself to his bedroom on the second floor.

Parents who subordinate their lives to their children, regardless of age, are irresponsible and will find that their children will have difficulty later on facing the realities and responsibilities of life outside the demand system they enjoy at home.

Are you steering your ship or are you a victim to the ill or fair winds of fate?

Are you a puppet dangling from the strings of your heredity and environment?

Are there a lot of things you have to do in life that have been forced upon you?

Do you have to go to work? No you don't. You could choose to lie in bed! There's always welfare.

Have to pay taxes? No you don't. You can earn too little to qualify... earn a lot but invest in tax deferral programs, try to beat the IRS, give up your citizenship, or go to prison!

Have to eat? No, you could starve if you chose to! You eat because you want to, because you've decided to, because it's profitable to your body.

I know many men who have to work late at the office—as if the company or their boss made them. I never have to work late. Sometimes I decide to work late because there are some important things I want to get done. I'd rather be home with my wife and family but I choose to work late at times because it's important to our financial plan for independence.

People who feel they *have* to do things usually forfeit many available options and alternatives and lose control of their lives in the bargain.

Responsible self-control is the path to mental health and, frequently, to physical health as well. Current research in biofeedback and meditation has verified human potential for control of brain wave emissions and body functions through specialized training and discipline. It is possible and may be practical for us to control our brain wave frequencies, pulse rate, threshold of pain, and other body functions as a means of positive health maintenance in the future.

Today, hundreds of biofeedback clinics are springing up in various parts of the country, teaching people how to raise their body temperatures in their extremities (finger-tips) in order to prevent the onset of migraine headaches; how to dilate their arteries to permit a greater blood flow to the heart and how to relax muscles and nerve endings.

There also has been a remarkable breakthrough in psychology, which was first led by Abraham Maslow prior to his death, and by Carl Rodgers, William Glasser, Viktor Frankl, and many other prominent humanists.

This new movement which is optimistic about human growth and potential is commonly referred to as Responsibility Psychology. It holds that irresponsibility and valuelessness lead to abnormal behavior, neuroses and mental deterioration.

Treatment for individuals suffering from these symptoms includes showing them that they need not be hung up on the past but are responsible for their present actions as well as their future behavior.

Psychiatrist Glasser and others have found that, when the neurotic individual is helped to assume personal responsibility, the prognosis for recovery is good. In case after case, they verify that responsible self-control leads to sound mental health.

The winning human being realizes that everything in life is volitional—even being alive. Everything "I decide to do"—nothing "I have to do."

You don't *have to* work, pay taxes, have babies, or even get up in the morning. You decide to do things because they are profitable to you and the best choice among the alternatives available to help you along toward your goals.

People who *have to* do things are irresponsible. They are not in control. They are puppets caught in the habit of letting life happen to them. They are the Losers.

Losers let it happen—Winners make it happen.

In his book, *Self-renewal*, John Gardner states that winning individuals do not leave the development of their potential to chance. They pursue it systematically, and look forward to an endless dialogue between their potentialities and the claims of life—not only the claims they encounter, but the claims they invent.

Daily, thousands of individuals are finding that there is a bright new world out there to be discovered and are demonstrating Gardner's statement that "We don't know that we've been imprisoned until we've broken out."

We are not only victims of habit. In a very real sense each of us becomes a prisoner of hundreds of restrictions of our own making.

Teenagers have a strong need to conform to the standards of their group. While they may feel that their special way of grooming is an act of independence, on the contrary, their styles and activities adhere very strictly to the peer code.

Those who refuse to be responsible for their own deeds, looking to others for their behavior cues, have not reached responsible maturity. Unfortunately, many adults spend their entire lives at this level of immaturity.

As we grow into adulthood, we make decisions that progressively narrow our opportunities and alternatives. We select only a few friends out of the thousands with whom we rub elbows, usually people with whom we agree, thus limiting our received input of fresh ideas.

We choose our educational level which in turn determines to a great extent our jobs and associates.

From day to day, comfortable in our safe, established ways, we seek the paths of least resistance.

The responsible people look at the shackles they have placed upon themselves by apathy and lack of imagination and, in a moment of truth, decry their predicament. Making a declaration of independence, they assert their option to choose and assume their rightful role of personal responsibility.

Famed anthropologist-sociologist, Margaret Mead, in her most recent book, calls "personal responsibility" our most important evolution, and the notion that we are the product of our environment, our biggest sin.

There should be a Statue of Responsibility standing in Los Angeles or San Francisco Harbor, to match the Statue of Liberty.

Without individual self-control and responsibility there can be no enduring liberty or freedom in our society. We will be free only as long as we can use freedom responsibly. The Law of Cause and Effect is forever the ruler.

Taking control of ourselves means taking the responsibility for making the best use of what we have—our minds, our talents and developed abilities, and that precious little time we have to spend on living. The choice is ours and it is here that personal honesty and responsibility determine whether we will win or lose our own Superbowl of life.

Earl Nightingale, in his radio broadcasts and writings, has reminded us through the years of one of the great natural laws of the universe: The Law of Cause and Effect. For every cause, there will be an effect nearly equal in intensity. If we make good use of our minds, skills, and talents, this will become illustrated in our outer lives. And, if we make the best use of our time, this too will give us a great advantage—for we know that scarcely one in a thousand individuals ever puts his or her time to anywhere near its potential good use.

This is being true to ourselves—taking control, accepting responsibility. In the final analysis, we are the only ones from whom we can steal time, talent and accomplishment. We are the only true field judges in our own daily Superbowls in life.

Let's imagine our great new Statue of Responsibility in San Francisco Bay on the site where the now-deserted Alcatraz stands. The inscription for all to see could fittingly be these words from "My Creed" by Dean Alfange:

"I do not choose to be a common man or woman. It is my right to be uncommon—if I can.

"I seek opportunity—not security. I do not wish to be

a kept citizen, humbled and dulled by having the state look after me.

"I want to take the calculated risk—to dream and build—to fail and succeed.

"I refuse to barter incentive for a dole. I prefer the challenges of life to the guaranteed existence—the thrill of fulfillment to the calm state of Utopia.

"I will not trade freedom for beneficence—nor my dignity for a handout. I will never cower before any master—nor bend to any threat.

"It is my heritage to stand erect, proud and unafraid—to think and act for myself—enjoy the benefits of my creations and to face the world boldly, and say—

"This I have done."

Winners get behind the wheel, firmly in the driver's seat. Winners take control of their thoughts, their daily routines, their goals, and their lives. They create their own horoscopes and astrological forecasts. They spend their time Winning ... knowing they have no time to Lose.

REVIEW

(Read this Positive Self-control Review several times over the period of one month to etch it in your memory.)

The *Positive Self-control* of a Total Winner is acceptance of one hundred per cent responsibility for causing the effects in his or her life. Winners realize they personally have the power to take control of many more aspects of their lives, both mental and physical, than were heretofore thought possible. They know that barring organic damage or congenital faults, self-control is the key to both mental and physical health and can contribute enormously to total well-being. Losers say: "I can't understand why life did this to me." Winners say: "I take the credit or the blame for my performance."

Instead of biorhythm computers, astrological signs, gurus, cults, and the federal government—*YOU* take the credit for determining, creating, making your own place in this world. You're in the driver's seat in your own life. In many respects, you've exerted control since you were born and cried for milk and a dry diaper. You can learn how to respond and adapt more successfully to the stresses of life by accepting responsibility today for causing your own effects. You alone hold the key to your reactions to people who want to rain on your parades. Remember, it's not so much "what happens" that counts in life; it's "how you take it." The real essence of Positive Self-control is that everything in life is volitional and that each of us has many more choices and alternatives than we are willing to consider. We even have control over body functions that we thought were purely involuntary. Winners really do make it happen for themselves.

Take Action Today for More Positive Self-control:

1. *Take the blame and the credit* for your position in life honestly and openly.

2. *Use the volition of "I've decided to,"* in place of the compulsion "I have to." *Use "I'm more comfortable doing this,"* in place of "I'm afraid to do that," the inhibition, as a condition for non-participation.

3. *Carry the affirmative motto: "My rewards in life—will reflect my service and contribution,"* with you in every daily transaction.

4. *Learn how to relax mentally and physically,* using meditation, mind relaxation, or biofeedback techniques—instead of external stimulants and depressants (unless they are prescribed by a competent physician for a specific organic health problem). A nearby university usually will offer the more legitimate ongoing mental and physical fitness programs.

5. *Set a specific time frame each week, preferably each day, to initiate action letters and action calls in your own behalf.* Don't wait for invitations to succeed—you'll go into the Losers' Hall of Fame as one of those almost-made-its with "permanent potential." Go for it! If someone has not responded to a letter from you within two weeks, send a follow-up mailgram or call. If there is still no response, take an alternate approach with someone else.

6. *"Action TNT—Action Today Not Tomorrow."* Carry this motto around with you and make it part of your lifestyle. Handle each piece of incoming mail only once. Answer phone calls as quickly as possible.

7. *Sit down and create your own best horoscope on paper.* List positive alternatives to habits that you seriously want to change. Seek out authorities with proven records of success after whom to model your winning habits.

8. *For the next 30 days, go all out in your current job.* Whatever you have chosen as your life's work, remember your job couldn't care less about you one way or the other— only you can take the initiative to give your job what it has deserved all along. Dedicate yourself just for one month, not for a lifetime, to giving your maximum effort to your job, your company, your routine and your service to others. At the end of that time, I think you'll find yourself renewing your dedication for another month.

9. *Invest in your own knowledge and skill development.* Since the only real security is the kind that's inside each of us, practice what Ben Franklin wrote: "If an individual empties his purse into his head, no one can take it from him." Seminars, books, tapes—take charge!

10. *Set your alarm a half-hour early tomorrow and leave it at the earlier setting.* Use this extra half-hour of your life to wake up and live. Use this time to answer the question— How can I best spend my time today on priorities that are important to *me*?

The Strangest Secret:
"We become
What we think about
Most of the time."
            —Earl Nightingale

CHAPTER 4

POSITIVE SELF-MOTIVATION

Antonyms:
Fear, compulsion, inhibition

Synonyms:
Desire for change, excitation, urge

Losers' Self-talk:
"I have to, I can't."

Winners' Self-talk:
"I want to, I can."

Proverb:
"Winners dwell on their desires, not their limitations."

Winners have desire. They are dissatisfied with the status quo. They want change for the better. There never was a Winner who didn't want to Win.

Scores of achieving people in every walk of life are all around us, yet few of us ever think of the long and arduous process that led them step-by-step to their goals. Who, for instance, remembers that Winston Churchill was a poor student, or that Althea Gibson came from the back-alleys of Harlem to the front court at Wimbledon.

They wanted something special for themselves—in spite of their early track records. In spite of their blood lines or their home lives—they wanted to Win.

Many people have the mistaken idea that personal motivation is an option—like an hors d'oeuvre which can be taken or left alone. But everything an individual does, whether positive or negative, intentional or unintentional, is the result of motivation.

Everyone is self-motivated—a little or a lot—positively or negatively.

Motivation is a much maligned, over-franchised, over-promoted, and misunderstood term. The word, "Motive" is defined as that within the individual, rather than outside, which incites him or her to action; an idea, need, emotion, or organic state that prompts to action.

Motivation is a force which moves us to action, and it springs from inside the individual. Defined as a strong tendency toward or away from an object or situation it can be learned and developed. It does not have to be in-born.

For too long, however, it has been wrongly assumed that motivation is extraneous—that it can be pumped in from the outside through incentives, pep talks, contests, rallies, and sermons. Such activities do provide concepts, encouragement and inspiration for individuals to turn on their creative powers—*but only if they want to*.

And that's the secret. Lasting change is effected only when the need for change is both understood and internalized. Until the reward or incentive has been interpreted and internalized, it has no motivating power.

Winners in life are people who have developed strong, Positive Self-motivation. They have the ability to move in the direction of goals they have set, or roles they want to play, and will tolerate little distraction.

In the face of discouragement, mistakes and setbacks, their inner drive keeps them moving upward toward self-fulfillment.

Motivation is an emotional state.

The great physical and mental motivators in life—survival, hunger, thirst, revenge, love, are charged with emotion.

Two key emotions dominate human motivation with opposite, but equally effective results—fear and desire.

Fear is the most powerful negative motivator. It is the great compeller and the great inhibitor. Fear restricts, tightens, panics, forces, and ultimately scuttles plans and defeats goals.

Desire, conversely, is like a strong, positive magnet. It attracts, reaches, opens, directs, and encourages plans and achieves goals.

Fear and desire are poles apart, and lead to opposite destinies. Fear looks to the past—desire to the future.

Fear vividly replays haunting experiences of failure, pain,

disappointment, or unpleasantness, and is a dogged reminder that the same experiences are likely to repeat themselves.

Desire triggers memories of pleasure and success, and excites the need to replay these and to create new winning experiences.

The consuming "prison" words of the fearful person are likely to be "I have to," "I can't," "I see risk," and "I wish."

Desire says, "I want to," "I can," "I see opportunity," and "I will."

Desire is that emotional state between where you are and where you want to be. Desire is a magnetic, positive tension.

Negative tension, induced by fear, creates stress, anxiety, sickness, and hostility; carried to extremes it can cause psychoses and death.

Positive tension, produced by desire, is like a bow pulled taut to propel the arrow to the bullseye.

In a totally tension-free state, you are either comatose or dead.

Viktor Frankl, noted psychiatrist and founder of the psycho-therapeutic school known as logotherapy, flatly states that what a person actually needs is not a tensionless state, but the striving and struggling for a goal that is worthy of him or her.

Mike Nichols, Broadway actor-producer, says "Nerves provide me with energy. They work for me; it's when I don't have them, when I feel at ease, that I get worried."

When you get "butterflies" in your stomach before a performance, accept them as butterflies. Butterflies are nice.

When they start to eat you, they are like moths. Moths in your stomach are not nice. They cause ulcers.

Winners respond positively to stresses in life, just as professional athletes, executives, educators, doctors, nurses, and homemakers respond successfully to stresses in their arenas.

One of the best guarded secrets in the kind of self-motivation practiced by high achievers and effective leaders is that, since we always move in the direction of what we are thinking of most, it is imperative to concentrate our thoughts on the condition we *want* to achieve rather than try to move away from what we fear or don't want. Simply stated, Winners focus on concepts of solutions rather than concepts of problems.

The mind cannot concentrate on the reverse of an idea. An excellent illustration of this statement is in the true story concerning one of the most exciting World Series baseball games of the 1950s between the New York Yankees and the Milwaukee Braves. Warren Spahn, the great Milwaukee Hall of Famer, was on the mound for the Braves. Elston Howard, the power-hitting catcher for the Yankees, was batting at the plate. It was the classic confrontation—late innings, pitchers' duel, man on base, deciding game of the series. The tension was paramount. The Milwaukee manager trotted out to the mound for a quick "motivation" conference with Spahn. "Don't give Howard a high, outside pitch—he'll knock it out of the park!" were the final words as the manager finished the pow-wow. Warren Spahn tried not to throw the ball high and outside. He tried to relax and aim low at the inside corner. Too late! Like a neon light the motivating image "high outside" was the dominant signal. It was a home run pitch.

After the game which almost (thanks to Eddie Matthews, Milwaukee pulled it out) lost the series for the Braves, Warren Spahn thought to himself, "I'll never again try to force my thought away from what I don't want, away from a feared result."

And so it is with all of life's daily confrontations. "Clean up your room, you little pigs!" say the fear motivating parents. And what do they get? You're right! A *pigsty*! And the kids say "Oink, Oink!"

Winners know that their actions will be controlled by their current obsessions.

Perhaps as much as any present day superstar in sports and in business, Jack Nicklaus, the golfing legend, personifies the quality of Positive Self-motivation by Desire as opposed to Fear. A veteran of the pro tour recently remarked, "Imagine the mind to be a quart jar. Jack Nicklaus makes sure the jar is always full of positive thoughts—intentions of hitting accurate, good shots. The rest of us tend to fill the jar at least halfway with negative thoughts. We're thinking *what can go wrong* with a shot, rather than *what should go right.*" Nicklaus' mind is so permeated with the task at hand there's no room for negatives. He controls every move to a specific end under conditions where most of our minds would be going a hundred ways at once. This tremendous ability to focus and concentrate on the currently dominant thought—on the winning action—is the mark of a winning superstar. And Jack Nicklaus has applied this action quality to his many successful business enterprises. He has proven that when one concentrates on doing one thing extremely well, it will take seed and grow and multiply into many diversified opportunities. Winners know that their actions will be controlled by their current obsessions.

Winners see risk as opportunity. They see the rewards of success in advance. They do not fear the penalties of failure.

The ennervating powers of fear are unfortunate, for individuals so dominated cannot act with volition and positive intent; rather, they go through life reacting, defensive and incapacitated. People who are dominated by stress are unable to change the world they live in—the world they live in alters them. It is a strange and sobering axiom that the thing we fear, we ourselves bring to pass.

Many years ago the English essayist James Allen wrote: "They who have conquered doubt and fears have conquered failure. Their every thought is allied with power, and all difficulties are bravely met and wisely overcome."

Desire is the perfect mental antidote for fear and despair.

Desire sparks activity, which burns up excess adrenalin in the system, keeps the mind busy and the hope of achievement alive. Inactivity breeds despondency, brings forth dark imaginings and distorts situations out of all proportion to reality. When fear begins to beg for attention, the Winner gets busy and things regain their proper perspective.

Norman Vincent Peale tells a wonderful true story about Maurice Chevalier who for many decades delighted audiences all over the world with his jaunty straw hat, crooning voice and whimsical smile. He was the debonair boulevardier, America's number one Frenchman.

Early during his brilliant career, he suffered a nervous breakdown just before he was to go on stage. He was ordered to rest in the southern part of France. "I'm a beaten man," he told the doctor. "I'm afraid of being a failure. There is no future for me now." He was advised to take long walks to repair his damaged nervous system. But the inner turmoil did not leave him. He was terribly afraid—he had lost all confidence.

After a time when the doctor thought the actor was ready for it, he suggested that Chevalier entertain before a small group in the village hall. "But," said Maruice, "I am terrified at the thought. What guarantee is there that my mind will not go blank again, that the dizziness will not return?" "There is no guarantee, but you must not be afraid of failing. You are afraid to step on a stage again, and so you are telling yourself that you are finished. But fear is never a reason for quitting; it is only an excuse. When winning individuals encounter fear, they admit it and go on despite of it. Don't be afraid to be afraid. Go on and perform even so."

Maurice suffered untold agony of fear before his appearance in that little town in front of those people, but he went on and performed very well. Joy welled up inside him. "I knew that I had not permanently conquered fear. But I admitted it and went on despite it. The idea worked!"

Since that evening six decades ago, Maurice Chevalier performed before huge audiences everywhere. "There have been many moments of fear," said the entertainer. "The gentle doctor was right; there is no guarantee. But being frightened has never made me want to quit."

Maurice added, "My own experience has taught me this. If you wait for the perfect moment when all is safe and assured, it may never arrive. Mountains will not be climbed, races won nor happiness achieved!"

And Maurice Chevalier achieved happiness. He never quit on life. He danced and sang his way into the hearts of millions for over eighty years. And his memory will linger on, for he was a person who won over himself. He never settled for defeat.

What have you settled for in life?

Have you hitched your wagon to a star or to someone else's wagon train?

There is a disturbing philosophical movement today that associates drive and initiative solely with materialistic power and gain.

The new so-called "leisure-time" culture assumes that motivation, money, politics, corporations, work, production, and success are synonymous obsessions of an over-industrialized, profit-oriented society.

While there does appear to be a growing obsession focused on the accumulation of non-essential personal possessions, this should not be confused with personal achievement and the pursuit of individual excellence.

Disregarding all material rewards for high achievement, there is a pure personal pleasure which comes with achieving the difficult. The emotional spin-off that accompanies performance of the unusual or challenging personal test can range from a quiet flow of self-esteem to outright exhilaration, and is reason enough for the pursuit of excellence.

After decades of quest, we now know that high achievers have a high degree of self-motivation. The enduring power that moves them to action comes from inside themselves.

Success is not reserved for the talented. It is not in the high I.Q. Not in the gifted birth. Not in the best equipment. Not even in ability.

Success is almost totally dependent upon drive, focus and persistence. The extra energy required to make an extra effort—try another approach—concentrate on the desired outcome—is the secret of winning.

Out of desire—the energy and will to win.

As Daniel Burnham said, "Make no little plans: they have no magic to stir your blood to action—make big plans, aim high in work and hope."

Get that urge to Win!

There's no time to Lose.

REVIEW

(Read this Positive Self-motivation Review several times over the period of one month to etch it in your memory.)

The *Positive Self-motivation* of Total Winners derives from two sources: (1) their self-expectant personal and world view and (2) their awareness that, while fear and desire are among the greatest motivators, fear is destructive while desire leads to achievement, success and happiness. With this in mind, they focus their thinking on the rewards of success and actively tune out fears of failure. Losers say: "I can't because. . . ." Winners say "I want to". . . and "I can!"

We are all self-motivated a little or a lot. Motivation is an inside job. Individuals are motivated by their fears, inhibitions, compulsions and attractions. They are pushed away from or pulled toward concepts and people who act as negative or positive magnets. Realizing the almost impossible task of moving away from negative concepts such as "fat," "poor," "sick," "klutz". . . winners focus on goals, desires, and solutions. Since most of our fears are based on dark imaginings, it is vital for us to dwell on our magnificent obsessions and desired results—to look at where we want to go, as opposed to that troubled place where we may have been or may still be hiding. People resist changing because it upsets their present security. People will change dramatically when it's a matter of life or death. And people will change happily and effectively. . . *when they want to*.

72

Take Action Today for
More Positive Self-motivation:

1. *Replace the word "can't" with "can" in your daily vocabulary. Can* applies to about 95 per cent of the challenges you encounter.

2. *Replace the word "try" with "will" in your daily vocabulary.* This is a form of semantics and simply establishes your new attitude of dwelling on things you *will* do, rather than on things you plan to *try*, with that built-in excuse in advance for possible failure.

3. *Focus all your attention and energy on the achievement of the objectives you are involved with right now.* Forget about the consequences of failure. Failure is only a temporary change in direction to set you straight for your next success. Remember, you usually get what you think of most.

4. *Make a list of five of your most important current wants* or desires, and right next to each . . . put down what the benefit or payoff is to you when you achieve it. Look at this list before you go to bed each night and upon awakening each morning.

5. *Seek and talk in person this week to someone who currently is doing what you want to do most, and doing it well.* This applies to skiing, acting, singing, speaking, hang gliding, selling, earning, or even being a good spouse or parent. Find an expert . . . get the facts; make a project of learning everything you can about Winners in the field. Take a course in it . . . get personal lessons; and generate excite-

ment by mentally seeing yourself enjoying the rewards of success.

6. *For every one of your goals make it a habit to repeat again and again, "I want to—I can," "I want to—I can."* Develop a simple, new, affirmative self-talk vocabulary about yourself.

7. *Paint the picture of what the achievement looks like and feels like*, when you are motivating others . . . and demonstrate your own confidence and belief in their ability to accomplish that given objective. Rather than saying "Firings will continue until morale improves" or "I'll divorce you unless you stop drinking" . . . motivate with "I've been observing your performance and want you to know how encouraged I am with your progress" or "There's a great play at the civic theater. Let's go there instead of the country club Saturday."

8. *Don't take counsel from your fears* and don't worry about them. They are part of being human. If any become obsessive—first get a thorough health check-up to determine if there is any organic association. Next, you might consider professional counsel involving relaxation, behavior modification and biofeedback techniques. Associate with other Winners. They'll help you overcome your fears.

9. *Give solution-oriented feedback when people tell you their problems.* When the problems are your own, focus on the immediate question—"What's the answer?"

10. *Concentrate all your energy and intensity, without distraction*, on the successful completion of your current project. Finish what you start.

Things usually work out my way
Because I create my daily horoscope
Out of my great expectations!

_____

CHAPTER 5

POSITIVE SELF-EXPECTANCY

Antonyms:
Pessimism, cynicism, despair

Synonyms:
Optimism, enthusiasm, hope

Losers' Self-talk:
"With my luck, I knew it would fail."

Winners' Self-talk:
"Good today, better tomorrow. Next time I'll get it right."

Proverb:
"That which you fear or expect most will surely come to pass; the body manifests what the mind harbors."

Every Winner can be identified easily because of his or her positive self-expectancy.

Winners expect to win. They know that so-called "luck" is the intersection of preparation and awareness.

They look at life as a very real game, but not as a gamble.

They expect to win for three key reasons:

1. *Desire*—they want to win.
2. *Self-control*—they know it is they who make it happen.
3. *Preparation*—they are *prepared* to win. They are ready. They have learned winning habits.

If an individual is not prepared, he or she simply does not see or take advantage of a situation.

Winners seem to be lucky because their positive self-expectancy enables them to be better prepared for their opportunities.

The single most outwardly identifiable trait demonstrated by a winning human being is that of positive self-expectation—which is pure and simple optimism.

The Winner in sports expects the best possible outcome in his or her particular event. The Winner sincerely believes that he or she is among the best, and all resultant energies are focused on proving it.

Doubters don't win. Winners don't doubt. Mark Spitz expected seven gold medals. Seven times during the Twentieth Summer Olympics he propelled himself through the water in his special swimming events. Incredibly, seven times he broke the existing world record. Before the games his confident manner and predictions of victory were construed by some as unwarranted conceit. What the public was witnessing can be more accurately described as the ultimate in Positive Self-expectancy.

Every individual tends to receive what he or she expects in the long run. You may or may not get what is coming to you, or you may or may not get what you deserve—but you will nearly always get what you expect.

Losers generally expect such occurrences as the loss of a job, bankruptcy, a dull evening, bad service, failure, and even ill health.

Perhaps the leading authority in the world today on the self-expectancy relationship between mind and body is Dr. Herbert Benson, Associate Professor of Medicine at the Harvard Medical School and Director of the Division of Behavioral Medicine at Boston's Beth Israel Hospital. He is the author of the best selling book, *The Relaxation Response* and his more recent work, *The Mind/Body Effect*, published by Simon & Schuster in 1979, documents the emotional relationship to many diseases.

In *The Mind/Body Effect*, Benson brilliantly explains the close interrelation between your mind and body in which thought processes lead both to disease and to good health. The concept of "Voodoo Death" is the extreme example of the potential negative effects of the mind on the body.

Voodoo, as we have come to understand it, is a set of religious practices said to have originated in Africa as a form of ancestor worship. Among Australian aboriginal tribes, witch doctors practiced the custom of "pointing the bone" whereby a magic spell was cast into the spirit of the victim. The purpose of such spells was to disturb the spirit of the victim so that disease and death would ensue.

The many instances of such death were dependent upon

both the victim's awareness of the spell cast and the victim's strong adherence to his society's belief systems.

One documented example in Dr. Benson's book tells of a young aborigine who, during a journey, slept at an older friend's home. For breakfast, the friend had prepared a meal consisting of wild hen, a food which the young were strictly prohibited from eating. The young man demanded to know whether the meal consisted of wild hen and the host responded "No." The young man then ate the meal and departed. Several years later, when the two friends met again, the older man asked his friend whether he would now eat a wild hen. The young man said he would not since he had been solemnly ordered not to do so by his elder tribesmen. The older man laughed and told him how he had been previously tricked into eating this forbidden food. The young man became extremely frightened and started to tremble. Within twenty-four hours he was dead!

In the Western world, many equivalents to voodoo death have been discovered in case histories.

"You will die," the fortune teller predicted, "when you are 43."

That prediction was made 38 years before when the fortune teller's client was five years old.

The little girl grew up with the awesome prediction on her mind—and died one week after her 43rd birthday, said a report in the British Medical Journal.

"We wonder if the severe emotional tensions of this patient superimposed on the physiological stress of surgery had any bearing upon her death," the doctors said.

They suggested she may have been frightened to death and said the case was that of an apparently healthy woman, a mother of five, who underwent a relatively minor operation. Two days later she was dead.

The doctors said that the night before the woman confessed to her sister—who knew of the fortune telling incident—that she did not expect to awaken from the anesthesia.

On the morning of the operation, the woman told a nurse she was certain she was going to die, but her fears were unknown to the doctors. An hour after the operation she collapsed and lost consciousness. A post mortem revealed extensive internal bleeding for which there was no reasonable explanation.

A spokesman for the British Medical Association said, "There is no medical explanation to account for this. It seems rather like the case of natives who die on the date and at the time the witch doctor predicts."

Consider, also, the death of Elvis Presley, the rock-star legend. He also died shortly before his 43rd birthday, of the same cause, at the same age, as did his mother. And he expected it to happen!

Careful studies of the life histories of thousands of widely differing people have persuaded competent scientists that the probability of "health changes"—sickness, accident, even pregnancy—can be predicted.

This finding is one of many results of current research in psychosomatic medicine—the study of the relationship between the mind and the body and how each affects the other. Scientists are learning that disease is not necessarily caused by germs—all persons have germs but only a few become ill. Instead, the cause of disease is closely linked with the way individuals react to life.

The line between stressful life changes, expectant anxiety and health changes seems to be associated with the body's immunity system, which makes antibodies to fight foreign material and germs. Situations which arouse fear and anxiety also suppress many body functions and they may suppress antibody production as well.

Distressful situations may also upset production of hormones which have a role in emotional balance. An emotionally upset individual is much more prone to accidents.

It is a fact that ulcers are not the result of what we ate, but what's eating us.

Arthritis and bursitis are often associated with rigid and mentally restrictive individuals.

Asthma is much more pronounced and lingering in a child that has been dwelled upon and overly protected by a doting parent—one who is the victim of "smother-love." An excellent treatment for this kind of asthma is a "parentectomy" at the Children's Asthmatic Hospital in Denver—remove the parent from the child and the child begins to breathe more easily again.

What does all of this have to do with self-expectancy and winning attitudes?

Simply this—mental obsessions have physical manifestations. You become that which you fear—you get what you suspect—you are that which you expect to be.

The power of the self-fulfilling prophecy is one of the most amazing phenomena of human nature.

What do you expect for yourself?

Another blue Monday or another one of those good days?

The Winner in life, believing in the self-fulfilling prophecy, keeps his or her momentum moving upward by expecting a better job, good health, financial gain, warm friendships, and success. The Winner sees problems as opportunities to challenge ability and determination.

Perhaps the greatest optimist I've ever met is the professional golfer, Lee Trevino. What a Winner!

Trevino says, "I'll admit I'm a money golfer. Everytime there are big stakes, I go for the purse."

When a lady asked for his autograph he noticed her gold pen. "My favorite color—gold," he quipped.

Lee Trevino is already a golf legend like Palmer, Nicklaus and Watson. He is one of the all-time top money winners in his seasons on the PGA tour. He is always in contention for the top spot.

There's something special about his game and the way he wins.

Lee Trevino does not have the powerful body of Jack Nicklaus. He does not have a picture swing. He doesn't look that good on the surface.

But he has a magnificent obsession—he expects to Win!

In an interview he said, "I won the Canadian Open and the U.S. Open. I'd like to go for the big three. I think I can win the British Open too!"

He did, sure enough!

Several years ago Lee Trevino caught pneumonia and was not fully recovered when the U.S. Open began. His doctor warned, "Better not play, you might get worse!" Trevino answered, "Might get better, might even win!" He almost won.

Some time ago, he was hit by lightning and had a long interruption in winning following back surgery. After he won the Canadian Open again he said, "That's more like me!"

What is it about this stocky, scrambling, self-approving, smiling little Latin that makes him so special? Lee Trevino is an incurable optimist. Don't try to tell him he's anything but the best, he just doesn't know any better.

He says, "You know they used to think I was a poor Mexican, but now they think I'm a rich Spaniard!"

You may call it arrogance. I call it confidence—brought about by the habit of enthusiasm. Optimism in action!

Positive Self-expectancy is just as important in the home as it is for athletes on the field, salesmen on the showroom floor, secretaries in the office. The enthusiasm of optimistic parents is contagious in the home. In their presence no one can remain neutral or indifferent. Their gentle good humor and ability to look on the bright side of life establishes an "espirit de corps" among the inner circle of loved ones. Children are infected by this wonderful penetrating outlook.

The winning individual knows that "bad luck" is attracted

by negative thinking, and that an attitude of optimistic expectancy is the surest way to create an upward cycle and to attract the best of "luck" most of the time.

When asked by a news reporter how she thought she would do in one of her early career swimming meets in the United States several years ago, 14-year-old Australian Shane Gould replied, "I have a feeling there'll be a world record today." She went on to set two world records in the 100- and 200-meter freestyle events.

When asked how she thought she would fare in the more testing, grueling 400-meter event, Shane replied,

"I get stronger every race, and besides . . . my parents said they'd take me to see your Disneyland if I win!"

She went to Disneyland with three world records. At 16 she held five world records and became one of the greatest swimmers of all time. She learned early about the power of self-expectancy.

Since all individuals are responsible for their own actions and cause their own effects, optimism is a choice. Achieving individuals—Winners—are "self-made," since their positive expectations make them what they are.

People shy away from negative, pessimistic, unbelieving Losers. They gravitate to positive, self-assured, optimistic Winners.

Optimism is like a forest fire, you can smell it for miles before you see it burning. Optimism is like fly paper. You can't help getting stuck to it.

Everybody loves a Winner. No one seems to swarm around a consistent Loser.

Optimism. Enthusiasm. Faith. Hope. Each is a synonym for Positive Self-expectancy.

What could a prisoner of war expect if not to go free?

What can you expect for yourself in life if not to Win?

Expect to Win—there is no time to Lose.

REVIEW

The most readily identifiable quality of a total winner is an overall attitude of personal optimism and enthusiasm. Winners understand the psychosomatic relationship—psyche and soma—mind and body...that the body expresses what the mind is concerned with. They know that life is a self-fulfilling prophecy, that a person usually gets what he or she actively expects. Losers say, "With my luck, I was bound to fail." Winners say: "I was good today, I'll be better tomorrow."

Your fears and worries turn into anxiety which is distressful—the production of certain hormones and antibodies changes; resistance levels are lowered and you become more vulnerable to disease and accident. Conversely, since your mind and body are trying to comply with your instructions and achieve a condition of "homeostasis" or balance, if your mental expectancy is healthy and creative your body will seek to display this general feeling with better health, energy and a condition of well-being. That is why many common maladies such as headaches, low back pain, ulcers, hives, shingles, asthma, and certain allergies are often identified with emotion rather than organic disturbances. By expecting the best, as a way of life, you are preparing yourself physically as well as mentally for the demands of winning.

Take Action Today for More Positive Self-expectancy:

1. *Use positive self-talk morning to bedtime.* "It's another good day for me." "Things usually work out my way." "I expect a great year." "Next time I'll do better." "We'll make it."

2. *Find something good in all of your personal relationships* and accentuate the blessings or lessons in even the most trying confrontations.

3. *Look at problems as opportunities*—make a list of your most pressing—the ones that block your professional and personal fulfillment. Write a one- or two-sentence definition of each problem. Now rewrite the definition, only this time view it as an opportunity or exercise to challenge your creativity and ingenuity. View the solution as you would if you were advising one of your best friends.

4. *Learn to stay relaxed and friendly* no matter how much tension you're under. Instead of participating in group griping, single out someone or something to praise. Instead of being unhelpfully critical be constructively helpful. When tension or anxiety enter the room, that's your signal to breathe slowly and deeply; to lower the tone and pitch of your voice, to sit back and relax your muscles and to respond calmly to problems with suggested solutions.

5. *Think well of your health.* Cure what's curable. Prevent what's preventable. Enjoy the rest.

6. *In projecting your own healthy condition to others, realize that your daily conversation is the automatic readout of your thoughts* and subconscious emotions. Use positive self-talk—"I'm feeling better now." "I feel young and vital." "I'm reaching my best weight." "I can feel the difference in my nutrition and exercise program."

7. *In dealing with children, in addition to ensuring proper health and medical treatment, focus the child's attention toward the reward or benefit of being well.* Too much attention paid to minor health irritations means there is a value to being sick like a child's version of "workmen's compensation" which, if habitual, can lead to a host of allergies, aches and exaggerated reactions.

8. *Expect the best from others, too!* Two of the keys to leadership are encouragement and praise. Vocalize, on a daily basis, your optimism and positive expectancy about your associates and family members. It's contagious.

9. *The best way to remain optimistic is to associate with Winners and optimists.* You can be realistic and optimistic at the same time by realistically examining the facts in a situation while remaining optimistic about your ability to contribute to a solution or a constructive alternative.

10. *Wake up happy.* Optimism and pessimism are learned behavioral attitudes. One of the best ways to develop Positive Self-expectancy is to start early in life or at least early on any given day. Wake up to music. Sing in the shower. Have breakfast with someone you like who is an optimist. Listen to a motivational tape on your way to work. Read educational and inspirational books and articles.

Your self-image
Is either your
Life-handicap
Or your
Auto-pilot for Winning!

CHAPTER 6

POSITIVE
SELF-IMAGE

Antonyms:
Dark imaginings, worries, neuroses

Synonyms:
Synthetic experience, visualization, creativity

Losers' Self-talk:
"I see me unattractive, average."

Winners' Self-talk:
"I see me changing, growing."

Proverb:
"What you think you see is what you get."

All Winners develop and actively think about *Positive Self-image*.

Winners act like Winners—imagining with pictures, feelings and words the roles they want to play. They give themselves a preview of coming attractions.

What you "see," is what you get.

Who you "feel," is who you are.

It is not what you "are" that holds you back, it's "what you think you are not."

Individuals behave, not in accordance with reality, but in accordance with their perception of reality. How the individual feels about himself or herself is everything, for all that he or she ever does or aspires to do will be predicated on that all-important concept which is the self-image.

The self-image is the fundamental key to understanding human behavior. If you change the self-image, you change the personality and the behavior. Dr. Maxwell Maltz, the great plastic surgeon and author of the best-seller, *Psycho-Cybernetics*, said that "The most important psychological discovery of this century is the discovery of the self-image."

Each of us, from childhood, weaves our own intricate web of self-images out of the beliefs born in response to every thought and experience, every humiliation and triumph—every loss and win.

Children's self-images are very pliable and susceptible

to external guidance and criticism. Young students who are treated as though they are mentally slow by teachers and parents will assume that they are, indeed, inferior to normal children.

You may recall the highly-publicized recent experiment conducted by a young primary grade school teacher upon her pupils. With approval from their parents, she told her class that "recent scientific reports had verified that children with blue eyes have greater natural learning abilities than children with brown eyes." She had them make up little signs designating them as "Blue Eyes" or "Brown Eyes" which were hung around their necks. After a week or so, the achievement level of the "Brown Eyes" group fell measurably, while the performance of the "Blue Eyes" improved significantly. She then made a startling announcement to the class. She had made a mistake! It was the "Blue or lighter eyes" who were the "weaker" students and the "Brown or dark eyes" who were the "stronger" students. Up went the image and achievement of the "Brown Eyes." Down, down came the performance of the "Blue Eyes." Talk about power of suggestion!

Just as with "stronger" and "weaker" students there is the image of the "stronger" and "weaker" sex. The male versus female syndrome. The woman's role in society used to be dominantly shaped by a restricted self-image as a result of associations of "weaker sex" with "lower," "slower," "lesser" potentials.

Today, the emergence of women in society as individuals is a major sociological movement. So-called "women's liberation" should be more appropriately labeled "women's elevation." As the self-image of woman is elevated, up goes the behavior and achievement, down come the self-imposed and outer-imposed barriers and out come the new opportunities for expression.

This may seem an over-simplification, but then in the

beginning we need to over-simplify things in order to understand them.

Each of us, male and female, has developed a self-image concerning every talent, every characteristic and every performance. "I'm a lousy cook—I can't boil an egg." "I'm a good dancer." "I have a great sense of humor." "I have a terrible memory." "I'm a sensitive, warm person." "I'm never on time." "A woman's place is in the home." "Men work, women wait." "I'm a true Leo." "I'm a born Loser." Each of us is controlled by these "mental pictures" we have formed. We cannot outgrow these limits we place on ourselves—we can only set new limits within which we must live.

Our self-image determines the kind and scope of person we are—it is our Life-controlling Mechanism.

Our self-image dwells at the subconscious level of thinking. Although the term "subconscious mind" is used loosely by laymen, it is probably more accurate to think of it not as a mind, but rather a mechanism or ability of the mind.

The "Judge": The conscious level of thinking, responsible for collecting information from the environment, storing it in the memory bank, and making rational decisions, can be compared to a judge.

The "Robot": The subconscious level of thinking, responsible for autonomic body control such as breathing and heart-beat, the storage of information in the so-called memory bank, and the goal seeking—can be compared to a robot, guidance computer or automatic pilot.

Guidance computers are devices which can be programmed to seek a target. They are installed in projectiles like the torpedo and the ballistic missile which are then guided by these highly sophisticated electronic systems that seek the target unerringly through the use of electronic data feedback. The human brain operates similarly but is far more marvelous and complex than any system man could ever invent.

For illustration, let's call the conscious level of thinking "The Judge," and the subconscious level of thinking "The Robot."

Their relationship: The first important point in this relationship is that the "Judge" cannot make a decision until clearing it with the "Robot" or subconscious. The "Robot" checks its memory bank, which houses the all-important self-image and instantaneously relays available data back to the "Judge" for action.

It would seem natural that your "Judge" would control your "Robot"—in a master/slave type relationship. Incredibly, the reverse is true!

The subconscious "Robot" controls the conscious "Judge" level of thinking. Action frequently takes place without consultation with the "Judge," but no action ever takes place without reference to the "Robot."

Information fed into your "Robot's" memory bank stays there. The billions of separate items of input over a lifetime are all there awaiting retrieval. They can never be willfully erased by you. They can be over-ridden or modified, but you're stuck with them for life.

For example, brain surgery by world authorities, Drs. Penfield and Roberts, at the Montreal Neurological Institute strongly supports this premise—literally confirms it as a fact. In their research, when brain cells were stimulated with an electrode, patients reported the sensation of re-living scenes from the past. The recall was so vivid that all details were present, including sounds, colors and odors. Not just remembering, but reliving the experiences!

During every moment of our lives we program our "Robot" to work for us or against us. Since it is only a mechanism, having no judging function, it strives to meet the objectives and goals we set for it, regardless of whether they are positive or negative, true or false, right or wrong, safe or dangerous. Its sole function is to follow instructions implicitly, based upon previous inputs, like a computer read-

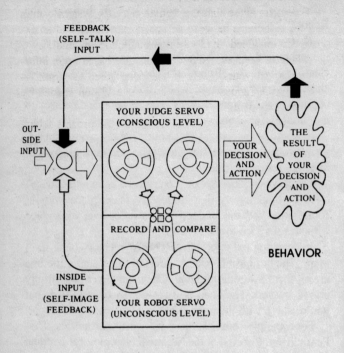

FEEDBACK
(SELF-TALK)
INPUT

OUT-
SIDE
INPUT

YOUR JUDGE SERVO
(CONSCIOUS LEVEL)

YOUR
DECISION
AND
ACTION

THE
RESULT
OF
YOUR
DECISION
AND
ACTION

RECORD AND COMPARE

BEHAVIOR

INSIDE
INPUT
(SELF-IMAGE
FEEDBACK)

YOUR ROBOT SERVO
(UNCONSCIOUS LEVEL)

SELF-IMAGE

ing its tape and responding automatically.

Scientists agree that the human nervous system cannot tell the difference between an actual experience and an experience imagined vividly, emotionally and in detail.

Many of your everyday decisions are based upon information about yourself which has been stored as "truth"— but is just a figment of your own imagination shaded by your environment.

A grammar schoolgirl has described the process which shapes the self-image perhaps as clearly as any psychologist could in her simple poem fashioned after "My Shadow."

My Robot

I have a little Robot
    That goes around with me.
I tell it what I'm thinking
    I tell it what I see.

I tell my little Robot
    All my hopes and fears.
It listens and remembers
    All my joys and tears.

At first my little Robot
    Followed my command
But after years of training
    It's gotten out of hand.

It doesn't care what's right or
    wrong
Or what is false or true
No matter what I try now
    It tells me what to do!

You are a slave to your subconscious "Robot," which houses your all-important self-image.

If you try to make a change in yourself at the conscious "Judge" level by using will power, the change usually will be only temporary.

Let us assume you have been a one-pack-a-day smoker for ten years and decide to give it up by good old-fashioned, teeth-gritting will power.

You go to the "Judge" and tell him you have given up smoking for good. The "Judge" wants to believe you, but is obligated to check all the evidence about your smoking record in the "Robot's" memory bank. The "Robot" checks the number of times you have tried to quit in the past and asks your self-image for a report. Your self-image has witnessed you as a smoker for the past ten years and testifies that you still "see" yourself inside as a smoker. Back up comes the "Robot's" report automatically, almost instantaneously, to the "Judge." The "Judge" who makes rational, conscious decisions based on testimony, has no alternative but to find you "guilty" of being a "smoker" who is likely to break his promise one day soon.

Whenever your "Judge" and "Robot" come in conflict, the "Robot" has the best chance of winning unless newly acquired fears or desires are strong enough to over-ride it.

Any permanent change in your personality or behavior, should first involve a change in your self-image, reinforced by a change in lifestyle. Then your long-range behavior or performance will follow.

Your behavior, personality or achievement level is usually consistent with your self-image.

A golfer's "handicap" makes a good illustration. You see yourself after so many rounds as a "lifetime" 18 handicap. You shoot consistently in the 90's.

One day you don't pay much attention to yourself and shoot a fantastic 36, or par, on the front nine. That's not like you, you're playing over your head. Considering your known handicap, and self-image as a golfer, what do you do on the back nine? Right! You adjust with a tree-, water- and sand-seeking ball! You get back to being "yourself." The tension finally goes away with a comfortable 55 on the back nine. Just about "right on" your self-image handicap.

Do you view your self-image as your life "handicap" or your "achievement mechanism"?

Are you a lifetime slave to your "Robot?"

You can't escape from your self-image! Oh, you can cop out with alcohol, drugs or mental depression. Losers take this trip every day! You can even get amnesia and forget the whole thing.

Winners control their self-image and change it as they desire. They elevate their self-image and enlarge their universe.

Winners know that worry, anxiety, hostility, and depression are negative, destructive users of their creative imaginations.

Winners dwell on and hold the self-image of that person they would most like to become.

They get a vivid, clear, emotional, sensory picture of themselves as if they had already achieved their goal.

Like children playing "Let's Pretend," they play the role of whomever they want to be. They know their little "Robots" can't tell the difference between "The real me" and "The one I see."

They see themselves standing in the Winner's Circle. They feel that solid weight of the gold medal around their necks. They hear the approval of the crowd. They smell the roses in the Rose Bowl. They touch the diploma in their hand. They feel the self-esteem of their personal achievement, however lofty or humble, in advance.

Winners feel like Winners. Winners "see" through the eyes of Winners.

What do you "see" for you today? Who will you be tomorrow? Think Win!

There is no time to Lose!

REVIEW

(Read this Positive Self-image Review several times over the period of one month to etch it in your memory.)

Winners are especially aware of the tremendous importance of their self-image—and of the role their imagination can play in the creation and up-grading of the self-image. They know the self-image acts as a subconscious life-governing device—that if in your self-image you can't possibly see yourself doing something, achieving something, you literally cannot do it! They also know the self-image can be changed since the subconscious is incapable of differentiating between a real success and a success *imagined* again and again vividly and in full detail. A Winner's self-talk is "I see myself changing, growing, achieving, winning!" Losers say, "They're *my* hangups, faults and stupidities . . . and I'm stuck with 'em."

Your behavior and performance usually are consistent with your self-image. Your self-image is an intricately woven concept made up of all your feelings, fears and emotional responses to each and every personal experience up to the present. As with any learned activity or skill, the self-image is housed at the subconscious or automatic level of thinking. What you perceive as real is filtered or shaded differently from what others perceive by your time-grown, robot-like self-image. What you imagine as being real, with frequency, becomes your version of reality. Winners imagine and fantasize that person they would most like to become—and the robot self-image reads the script, memorizes it and acts accordingly.

Take Action Today for More Positive Self-image:

1. *Go for a walk on the beach or in the country or park and recall your childhood play*. Dust off and "oil" your imagination. It rules your world.

2. *Set aside 20 to 30 minutes a day*, whether commuting to and from your place of business, at lunch, or in the morning or evening. As you relax during this time imagine yourself achieving and enjoying your most personal desires. See them as if you were previewing three television shorts. Picture yourself in one sequence achieving a professional triumph (imagine the award ceremony, promotion announcement or bonus payment). Picture yourself in another scene involving family happiness (imagine a special reunion or an outing together). Picture yourself in another setting in which you alone are relishing a personal victory (imagine a club tennis or golf championship or a weigh-in at the health club). Get the actual sensation of each event and how good it feels to experience each one.

3. *Read a biography this month*—and each month—the life story of someone who has reached the top in your profession, in your major hobby or just someone you admire. As you read, imagine yourself as the person you are reading about.

4. *While you relax, visualize your own imagined triumphs*. Listen to soft mood music in the background. The process of relaxing, plus the music will open the subjective window

in your subconscious level of thinking and make you most receptive to your own creative images.

5. *If you spend time around young children, become a story teller* using your imagination for a good, old-fashioned ghost story or science fiction tale once a week before bedtime.

6. *Limit your television viewing to stimulating, special shows*. If you just watch television as a habit, tunnel vision will set in and creative imagination will vanish. The same goes for your children!

7. *Take a deep relaxation, meditation, auto-suggestion, or biofeedback training program*. Develop the ability to "daydream" through this training so that you can smell the salt air, hear the waves lap at the side of the boat, see the sail full on the wind and the gulls on the wing and feel the exhilaration of ocean sailing as if it were really happening.

8. *Develop the habit of listening to educational and inspirational cassette tapes* while you are driving and before retiring in the evening. Listening sparks the imagination, and as in learning a foreign language, promotes retention of the subject permanently in your memory.

9. *Write a two-page resume of your professional and personal assets* as if you were going to apply for the job of a lifetime. Instead of past experience, list your maximum current potential and ultimate future growth potential. Read this two-page autobiography every week, revise it every two months, and show it only to those individuals whom you believe can and will help you toward your goals.

10. *Since the self-image is the visual, conceptual display of self-esteem*, take stock this weekend of those images with

which you display yourself: clothes, auto, home, garage, closet, dresser drawers, desk, photos, lawn, garden, etc. Make a priority list to get rid of all the clutter and sharpen up all the expressions of your life.

I'm gonna fly from my cocoon
And put my footsteps on
  the moon
All I've ever hoped to be
Is free to be that person . . . me!

CHAPTER 7

POSITIVE SELF-DIRECTION

Antonyms:
Aimless, non-specific, wandering

Synonyms:
Goal-seeking, purpose-oriented, cybernetic

Losers' Self-talk:
"I can't decide."

Winners' Self-talk:
"I have a game plan."

Proverb:
"No wind blows in favor of a ship without a destination."

Winners in life—those one in one hundred people—are set apart from the rest of humanity by one of their most important developed traits—*Positive Self-direction*. They have a game plan for life.

Every winner I have ever met knows where he or she is going day by day . . . *every* day.

Winners are goal and role oriented. They set and get what they want—consistently.

They are self-directed on the road to fulfillment.

Fulfillment or success has been defined as the progressive realization of goals that are worthy of the individual.

The "human" system is goal-seeking by design and, using a very basic analogy, may be compared to a homing torpedo system or an automatic pilot.

Set your target and this self-activated system, constantly monitoring feedback signals from the target area and adjusting the course setting in its own navigational guidance computer, makes every correction necessary to stay on target and score a hit.

Programmed incompletely, non-specifically or aimed at a target too far out of range, the "homing torpedo" will wander erratically around until its propulsion system fails or it self-destructs.

And so it is with each individual human system in life.

Set a goal and this self-motivated system, constantly monitoring self-talk and environmental feedback about the goal and adjusting the self-image settings in its subconscious robot achievement mechanism, makes every decision necessary to reach the goal.

Programmed with vague random thoughts, or fixed on an unrealistic goal too far out of sight, the "human system" will wander aimlessly around its world until it wears itself out, or until it self-destructs.

Winners are people with a definite purpose in life. Losers are people who wander aimlessly through life or self-destruct.

No one has given more clarity to the "human necessity for purpose" than Dr. Viktor Frankl, currently on staff at the United States International University in San Diego, California, and lecturing world-wide.

A psychiatrist in Vienna at the outbreak of World War II, Frankl was a prisoner in Nazi concentration camps for the duration of the war. Frankl arrived at his conclusions about *Man's Search for Meaning* (the title of his classic book on the subject), experiencing three years of horror in such death camps as Auschwitz and Dachau.

Observing himself and his comrades stripped of literally everything—families, professions, possessions, clothing, health, and dignity, he gradually developed his concepts concerning human purpose. Narrowly escaping the gas chambers and death by brutality many times, Frankl studied the behavior of both captors and captives with a curious detachment, and lived to put his observations in writing. We in America have been reminded of the impact of these human sufferings in timeless motion picture and television dramatizations such as *Holocaust*.

Perhaps more than any other authority on human behavior, Frankl's knowledge is first-hand and springs from objective evaluations of destitute humans living with the daily probability of death. These experiences enabled him to make a sharp departure from the theories of Sigmund Freud. For example, Freud taught that individuals differed in outlook and attitude while healthy, but that if humans were deprived of food, their behavior would become more and more uniform as they resorted to the level of their basic "animal-like" instincts. But Frankl states, "In the concentration camps we witnessed to the contrary; we saw how, faced with the identical situation, one man degenerated while another attained virtual saintliness."

He noticed that men were able to survive the trials of starvation and torture when they had a purpose for their existence. Those who had no reason for staying alive died quickly and easily.

The ones who lived through Auschwitz (about one in twenty) were almost without exception individuals who had made themselves accountable to life—there was something they wanted to do or a loved one they wanted to see.

In the death camps, inmates told Frankl that they no longer expected anything from life. He would point out to them that they had it backward. "Life was expecting something of them. Life asks of every individual a contribution, and it is up to that individual to discover what it should be."

The response to the challenges of life—purpose—is the healing balm that enables each of us to face up to adversity and strife.

"Where there is life, there is hope."

"Where there are hopes, there are dreams."

"Where there are vivid dreams, repeated, they become goals."

And goals become the action plans and game plans that Winners dwell on in intricate detail—knowing that achievement is almost automatic when the goal becomes an inner commitment.

What kind of goals are you committed to?

For many people—the thousands of Losers in daily life—getting through the day is their goal and as a result, they generate just enough energy and initiative to get through the day. Their goal is to watch television—soap operas by day, cops and robbers and situation comedies by night—having no goals of their own, they sit in a semi-stupor night after night with tunnel vision and watch TV actors and actresses enjoying themselves earning money, pursuing *their* careers and *their* goals.

Since we become what we think of most of the time, whatever we are thinking of now, we are unconsciously moving toward the achievement of that thought. For an alcoholic, this could be the next drink—for a drug addict, the next fix—for a surfer, the next wave. Divorce, bankruptcy, illness are all goals spawned out of negative attitudes and habit patterns.

If your goal is to retire, you'd better think twice, because true retirement is lying horizontally in a box with a lily in your hand.

There have been recent studies conducted by the insurance industry concerning retired military officers and businessmen who were looking forward to retiring and just doing nothing after 30 years of hard work. Do you know that they live about four to seven years in retirement? Not much time to enjoy their pensions and just doing nothing!

We all have the potential and the opportunity for success in our lives. It takes just as much energy and effort for a bad life as it does for a good life.

And yet, millions of us lead unhappy, aimless lives—existing from day to day, year to year, confused, frustrated, in a prison of our own making. Losers are people who have never made the decision that could set them free. They have not decided what to do with their lives, even in our free society.

They go to work to see what happens and you know what happens—they spend all their time making someone else's goals come true.

Thomas Carlyle and Earl Nightingale both compare human beings with ships. About 95 per cent can be compared to ships without rudders. Subject to every shift of wind and tide, they're helplessly adrift. And while they fondly hope that they'll one day drift into a rich and successful port, they usually end up on the rocks or run aground. But those five per cent who win, who have taken the time and exercised the discipline to decide on a destination and to chart a course, sail straight and far, reaching one port after another, and accomplishing more in just a few years than the rest accomplish in a lifetime.

Every sea captain knows his next port of call, and even though he cannot see his actual destination for fully 99 per cent of his voyage, he knows what it is, where it is and that, barring an unforeseen catastrophe, he'll surely reach it if he keeps doing certain things a certain way each day.

Winners in life start with lifetime goals. What do I stand for? What would I defend to the end? What would I want people to say about me after I am gone?

Winners know how important time-priority goals are. A five-year plan. A one-year program. A six-month campaign. A summer project.

But most of all, Winners know that the most important time frames are the groups of minutes in every day. Most people waste most of their waking hours every day going through the motions, chatting idly, shuffling papers, putting off decisions, reacting, majoring in minors, and concentrating on trivia. They spend their time in low priority tension-relieving, rather than high priority goal-achieving activities.

Since they fail to plan, they are planning to fail by default.

Most people spend more time planning a party, studying the newspaper, or making a Christmas list, than they do in planning their lives.

Winners set their daily goals the afternoon or evening

before. They list on paper in a priority sequence at least six major things to do tomorrow.

And when they start in the morning they go down the list, checking off the items they accomplish, adding new ones and carrying over into the next day's itinerary, those they did not complete.

What would happen if you did your grocery shopping without a list? You'd see all the packaged TV advertised displays, a potpourri of irresistible goodies and items. Count Chockula, Frankenberries, White Tornadoes, Twinkies, Star Wars T-shirts, and Farrah Fawcett, Bionic Woman, Bad News Bears decals and puppets. You'd be overwhelmed with goals you didn't set, didn't need and didn't really want.

Winning Self-direction is setting goals that are realistic and profitable to you and your family.

They should be specific. The mind, which operates like a homing torpedo or automatic pilot, is a robot computer— it gets what you set. It can't function properly without specific data. It can't relate to nebulous, vague or general terms like "happiness," "wealth," or "health." It does respond to $3,000 a month, a new car, a desired weight of 175 for a man or 120 pounds for a woman, and blood pressure of 118 over 88.

The secret to Positive Self-direction is in *establishing a clearly defined goal, writing it down*, and then dwelling on it morning and night, with words, pictures and emotions, as if you had already achieved it.

And since your robot self-image cannot tell the difference between something that is rehearsed or synthetically experienced and something that is real, you will move in the direction of your goal, whatever it is, as though it were already a part of your life.

We do become what we think about most. And no wind blows in favor of a ship without a destination.

The man without a purpose is like a ship without a rudder.

"One ship sails East, another West, by the selfsame winds that blow. 'Tis the set of the sail and not the gale, that determines the way they go.

"Like the winds of the sea are the ways of time, as we voyage along through life. 'Tis the set of the soul that determines the goal; And not the calm or the strife."

Get behind the helm. Plan the work and work the plan. A day at a time. Decide now on your goals. Force your goals into your subconscious with unrelenting practice—daily rehearsal.

See yourself achieving them one by one. Make winning your game plan in life in the time you have remaining. And Win today because . . .

There is no time to Lose!

REVIEW

(Read this Positive Self-direction Review several times over the period of one month to etch it in your memory.)

Winners in life have clearly defined, constantly referred to, game plans and purposes. They know where they're going every day, every month, every year. Their objectives range all the way from daily priorities to lifetime goals. And when they're not actively pursuing their goals, they're thinking about them—hard! They know the difference between goal-achieving acts and those which are merely tension-relieving . . . and they concentrate on the former. Winners say, "I have a plan to make it happen. I'll do what's necessary to get what I want." Losers say, "I'll try to hang in there—muddle through the day somehow."

Purpose is the engine that powers our lives. Everyone has purpose. For some it is to eat, for others it is to get through the day, and for others it is revenge or getting even. For Winners—personal growth, contribution, creative expression, and sharing, loving relationships seem to be common goals that make them such uncommon people. Clearly defined, written goals are the tools which make purpose achievable. Since the mind is a specific bio-computer it needs specific instructions and directions. The reason most people never reach their goals is that they don't define them, learn about them or ever seriously consider them as believable or achievable. In other words, they never set them. They fail by default. Winners can tell you where they are going, approximately how long it will take, why they are going, what they plan to do along the way, and who will be sharing the adventure with them. Get a game plan for life!

Take Action Today for More Positive Self-direction:

1. *What are your lifetime goals?* What do you stand for, what do you want your children to tell their children about you? Jot down a one-page brief.

2. *What are your priority goals* in groups of years. For the next *five* years write one major goal in each of the eight following areas: career, physical, family, personal attitude, financial, public service, educational, and entertainment.

3. *List your top priority goals for next year* using the same eight categories as in Number 2. above. After reviewing your progress toward this year's goals on December 31 or January 1 set your annual goals for next year.

4. *Use a large desk-top calendar* and set your time priority goals for *next month*. What will you do, where will you go, with whom will you communicate during the next thirty days in order to achieve your annual goals?

5. *Use a pocket week-at-a-glance type calendar and set activities for next week* that will help achieve your monthly goals. Review it and check off accomplishments each morning and evening.

6. *Use an 8½" by 11" lined folio pad and set the most important goals of all—your daily goals for tomorrow.* Write down at least ten priority projects for tomorrow at

the close of each working day. Review it just before you go to bed and early the following morning. As on a grocery shopping list, check off each item as accomplished and carry over into the following day those that were not completed.

7. *Make special effort to sit down and draft your financial game plan* which will fuel your personal growth cycle. Select your income goal at retirement age, giving effect to inflation probabilities, and determine the annual savings and investment yields you will have to generate from now on to build the assets that will provide the income you need. Check your insurance against income loss, check your emergency and contingency savings and plan your monthly budget to provide a discretionary surplus for a savings plan, rather than disposable income to spend on unnecessary gadgets of convenience.

8. *For each of your goals, assemble support material,* news articles, books, tapes, pictures cut out of magazines, consumer reports, cost estimates, color swatches, samples, etc. Review these often.

9. *Review your goals with Winners*—and experts who have proven records of success in actually accomplishing what you have set out to do. Differentiate between those who want to *sell* you and those who are sincere in wanting to help you. One of the best ways is to pay someone strictly for advice and counsel, someone with no end product or other service to sell.

10. *For best results in goal achieving use these basic rules*:
   (a) Set *short-range* goals (day, week, month, six-months)
   (b) Set *lower-level* goals (relatively easy to accomplish)
   (c) Set *incremental* goals (little by little, part of the big objective)

(d) Get *group* reinforcement (regularly consult a support group interested in the same achievement)

(e) Ceremonialize the achievement (certificate, reward, dinner, trip, recreation, new clothing, etc.)

Everything in life
Is what you make it . . .
It's not what is that counts,
It's how you take it!

CHAPTER 8

POSITIVE SELF-DISCIPLINE

Antonyms:
Repetitive error, inconsistency, discouragement

Synonyms:
Achievement simulation, drill, practice

Losers' Self-talk:
"I have a habit of losing."

Winners' Self-talk:
"I practice winning mentally within, when I am without."

Proverb:
"Habits begin as harmless thoughts—like flimsy cobwebs—then, with practice, become unbreakable cables to shackle or strengthen our lives."

Winners practice *Positive Self-discipline*. Self-discipline is practice!

Self-discipline "puts your money where your mouth is."

Self-discipline dares you to place a bet on yourself.

Self-discipline begins where "lip service" ends.

All other "winning qualities" in this book are absolutely worthless without self-discipline.

You may be self-motivated by desire. You may feel you are in control. You may expect to go to the moon. You may imagine yourself on the moon. But you will never even get near the launching pad without persistent self-discipline.

But up to now, it all seemed so simple. You tell your little "Robot subconscious achievement mechanism" that you want a new self-image and—zap—up we go.

Well, there's a little more effort involved. You have been the way you are for some time now. And every day, your actions and reactions usually confirm and support your present self-image. You constantly talk to yourself every minute you are awake maintaining and justifying "who you are" today. This has gone on for years.

Your little Robot has matured into a "control room" full of some very big habits!

Habits start out as off-hand remarks, magazine advertisements, friendly hints, experiments—like flimsy cobwebs with little substance. They grow with practice, layer upon layer—thought upon thought—fused with imagination and emotion until they become like steel cables—unbreakable. Habits are attitudes which grow from cobwebs into cables that control your everyday life.

Self-discipline alone can make or break a habit. Self-discipline alone can effect a permanent change in your self-image and in you. Self-discipline achieves goals.

Many people define self-discipline as "doing without." A better definition for discipline is "doing within." Self-discipline is mental practice—the commitment to memory of those thoughts and emotions that will override current information stored in the subconscious memory bank. And through relentless repetition, the penetration of these new inputs into our "Robot achievement mechanism" resulting in the creation of a new self-image.

Self-discipline through concentrated self-talk is needed even when a sudden, dramatic physical change takes place outwardly deserving of a new self-image.

Dr. Maxwell Maltz found that after plastic surgery many individuals take about three weeks to become accustomed to their new faces. Gradually they begin to feel comfortable with their new "selves." Sometimes, however, the old self-image is so ingrained that even those who have been transformed from homely people to attractive ones have emotional difficulty in accepting the new self.

Dr. Maltz refers to one of his patients who had come to him with a pronounced, unattractive hook nose and whom he altered to have a facial appearance not unlike Eva Gabor's, with a perfectly shaped nose. Admiring the results in front of a mirror, Dr. Maltz happily queried, "How do you like the new, beautiful you?"

She replied coldly, "I don't see much improvement. I still feel ugly!"

Another overt illustration of the tenacity of the time-grown self-image is in the study of amputees. In reality—physically, consciously and at the judgment level of think-

ing—the limb is gone. But, for several weeks, sometimes
longer, the patient will experience pain, itching or tingling
in hands or feet that are no longer there. During the night
some try to get out of bed and walk, only realizing after
they have fallen that they are legless. The image lingers on,
long after reality is changed!

If it requires several weeks to mentally accept a new self-
image brought about by a permanent physical change—
consider the self-discipline required to change your image
of reality totally from the inside.

Self-discipline is telling yourself over and over with words,
pictures, concepts and emotions that you are winning each
important personal victory now.

Winners practice on and off the playing field, in and out
of the office. They create or simulate each experience they
want.

Every Winner I've ever met in every walk of life, male
or female, uses the technique of mental simulation every
day in his or her imagination.

I met a world champion Russian figure skater and she
said, "I rarely fall because I practice each sequence in my
imagination at night with my eyes closed, and could successfully perform my entire routine blindfolded with no
hesitation."

I sat next to a gentleman on a recent flight to Chicago
who was making a weird, high-pitched humming sound with
his eyes closed. I turned the overhead air nozzle on his face
and asked him if he wanted me to call the stewardess to
come to his aid. He retorted indignantly, "I beg your pardon.
I am an oboist for the Chicago Symphony Orchestra and I
am practicing for tonight's performance. Now if you will
excuse me. . . ."

Did you ever see former Olympic champion high jumper
Dick Fosbury do the famous "Fosbury Flop"—a backward
swan dive over a 7 foot 3 inch bar? If you have, did you
notice that he rocked back and forth for several minutes

with his eyes closed before charging straight ahead for his backward leap? Dick Fosbury "saw" himself successfully going over the bar in his mind while rocking back and forth before each jump.

French skier Jean-Claude Killy won the giant slalom in his imagination first. Mental simulation is an excellent way to practice skiing and gain confidence. Feet together, weight properly balanced, correct knee position, down the fall line, watch for moguls, feel the pure, crisp snow, the wind, the speed, the exhilaration of doing it all yourself. For champions, it's the winning edge. For beginners, a great way to conquer fear. After all, in your imagination, you never fall!

Reader's Digest some years ago told of a class of high school basketball players with similar skills who were divided into three separate groups to conduct an experiment. Group I was told not to practice shooting free throws for one month. Group II was told to practice shooting free throws in the gym every afternoon for one hour for one month. Group III was told to practice shooting free throws in their imagination every afternoon for one hour for one month.

Group I, with no practice for a month, slipped from a 39 per cent to a 37 per cent free throw average. Group II, who practiced in the gym increased from a 39 to a 41 per cent average. The players in Group III, who practiced in their imaginations went from a 39 to a 42.5 per cent average!

Ridiculous! How could your free throw average improve more from practicing in your imagination than from actual practice with the ball and basket in the gym? Simply because in your imagination you never miss! Another swisher and another—practice makes perfect. In the gym, when you make three in a row, your self-talk might be, "I hope I can continue" or "I wonder when I'll miss" or "that was a lucky one." In the gym, when you miss one or two, your self-talk might be, "Get it in, you klutz!" or "There I go again." Your self-talk after a performance usually conforms to your current self-image and keeps your aim locked near your present performance.

Tennis stars visualize, a few micro-seconds before their rackets make contact with the ball, where the next shot will be placed.

Golfing greats like Tom Watson and Gary Player, when they upon rare occasions hit a shot badly, replay the shot in imagination and with the same club—only this time they play it just right.

Practice, practice, practice. So what else is new? Anyone can write a book filled with world record holders and their achievements, and give credit to practice, practice, practice!

Well, everyone unknowingly practices every day. Look at all the "duffers" at the driving range. It's more like an unguided missile range! It's a dangerous place, even behind the tee near the snack bar. We spend most of our time practicing our bad habits rather than our good ones or even looking for good ones.

We are relentless in our expertise at becoming accomplished Losers. Warning!—Losing is habit forming and may be dangerous to your mental and physical health.

Winners simulate winning. They practice, as if they are first even if their challenge is a first for mankind.

Astronauts are living examples of winning self-discipline. Look at the Apollo crews—playing "let's pretend we are going to the moon." No one had ever done it before! Who, other than Jules Verne, Ray Bradbury or Isaac Asimov really dreamed it possible?

Astronauts are masters at mental simulation. They practice bobbing up and down in a rubber raft at sea, responding to the feeling of "weightlessness" to be experienced in outer space. They practice on the desert with a simulated Lunar Excursion Module, as if they were landing it on the surface of the moon.

Hour after hour, month after month, they memorize and simulate the exact theoretical steps with hundreds of critically vital sequences that NASA scientists have imagined would take them safely to the moon and back.

Then, Neil Armstrong takes the first giant step and transmits his reactions back to Mission Control in Houston, "It was beautiful, just like our drills." On a later moon expedition Apollo Captain Conrad commented, "It's just like old home week. I feel like I've been here many times before. After all, we have been rehearsing this moment for the past four years!"

"So what?" you say. Look at the billions of dollars of government resources and brilliant minds backing up the Space Program. What about some "Winners" who use self-discipline to win with no help and no financial support?

The most amazing breakthrough in discovering the incredible ability of the mind to store and retrieve data in large quantities and with near-perfect clarity has been the work by Dr. Georgi Lozanov, a leading psychiatrist in Sofia, Bulgaria.

Dr. Lozanov has developed a method of cue-reinforced learning which we will be hearing about on a world-wide basis in the 1980s as "Suggestology" or "Suggestopedic Learning."

Originating in Bulgaria, and monitored by the United Nations, this innovative program reteaches the broader areas of the mind and brain by combining the techniques of relaxation, psychology of suggestion, psycho-drama, and repeated listening. Dr. Lozanov's experiments with hyper-rapid learning of foreign languages have stunned educators throughout the world . . . by enabling first grade students to learn more than a thousand words of a foreign language in a single day! Plus, they taught first graders complicated algebraic equations and concepts so that they understood as well as learned the techniques of solving problems that would test most high school seniors. And these were just average first graders, six years old!

History books and record books are full of Winners in

life who have made it on their own by sheer determination and "guts" against all the odds.

Winners are people who can "do within" while they are "doing without."

Helen Keller, Pancho Segura, Maureen Connolly, Glen Cunningham, O. J. Simpson, Tom Dempsey, Eleanor Roosevelt, Mahatma Gandhi, Martin Luther King, Albert Schweitzer, even John Milton, and Lord Byron—read their biographies; self-discipline is a common thread.

More recent, and certainly more emotionally illustrative, examples of winning self-discipline have been exposed through the experience of our POW's returning from Viet Nam.

Through the joyful heart-rending, tearful reunions with families and country, did you get a good look at the self-discipline in action?

Did you hear or read about the prisoners' habit patterns and practice sessions during their three to seven years of deprivation and boredom?

What would you do if you were locked up with no end in sight? Sleep? Read? Get depressed a lot? Feel sorry for yourself? Resent the folks back home?

Or would you, as most of them did, make prison a self-improvement retreat?

Several of our POW's made guitars out of wooden sticks and strings. Although their crude instruments made no sound at all, those who knew how to play practiced from memory, listening in their imaginations. They taught each other many new chords, finger positions and songs. Some who had never held a guitar before, are now accomplished guitarists. Seven years is a long time!

Other POW's at the Hanoi Hilton fashioned piano keyboards by taking a flat board and pencil-sketching the keys actual size. Although their Steinways were silent and unplayable, they practiced day after day and enjoyed their favorite selections.

Physical fitness abounded in the prison camps. When there was nothing else to do, they did sit-ups. One POW now holds the world's record—4,500 without resting.

Air Force Colonel George Hall played an imaginary round of golf each day during his seven years as a POW in North Vietnam. Those mental exercises paid off when he got back to the real thing. After seven golf-less years and less than one month after his release, he was back in form, playing to his four-stroke handicap in the Pro-Am preliminary to the $125,000 Greater New Orleans Open.

Many American POW's taught each other a foreign language. Many of our returnees now speak three languages fluently.

There were no Bibles at the Hanoi Hilton, so the POW's pooled their memory banks and reconstructed hundreds of the most significant passages for their Sunday worship services.

The POW's taught each other skills from rote memory, discussed and re-discussed boyhood experiences of mutual interest and value, created complete "mental" diaries while in solitary confinement, invented hundreds of money-making ideas and, perhaps most importantly, gained perspective by remembering and sharing ideals that are the foundation of their country's greatness.

Self-discipline in action! When Winners are without, they work and practice to toughen themselves to the task. They know that the imagination is the greatest tool in the universe. It *is* the universe of a prisoner of war.

Winners never quit. Winners never give up.

Winners pick themselves up, dust themselves off, and do it all over again...better!

Discipline yourself to win. Practice "within" when you are "without." Practice before you go to sleep. Practice after you wake up. Practice in the shower. Practice in the car.

Make Winning your habit!

There's no time to Lose.

REVIEW

(Read this Positive Self-discipline Review several times over the period of one month to etch it in your memory.)

Positive Self-discipline is the ability to practice *within*. Winners are masters of the art of simulation. Like astronauts, championship athletes, great stage performers, skilled surgeons, and truly professional executives and salesmen, they practice flawless techniques in their minds over and over, again and again. They know that thought begets habit and they discipline their thoughts to create the habit of superb performance—the mark of a Total Winner. You may have desire. You may feel you are in control. You may expect to go to the moon. But you will never even get near the launching pad without persistent self-discipline. Most people forget the simple routine for learning a skill or habit: Desire, Information, Assimilation, and Repetition. We learned how to walk, drive, type, fly, speak a foreign language, ski, act in a play, etc. Why is it so difficult for us to apply learning to our most important life goals? Everything is habit-forming if it is repeated! Self-discipline alone can make or break a habit. Self-discipline alone can effect a permanent change in your self-image and in you. Self-discipline is the winning edge that achieves goals. Self-discipline is mental practice—the commitment to memory of those thoughts and emotions that will override current information stored in the subconscious memory bank. And through relentless repetition, the penetration of these new inputs into our "Robot achievement mechanism" resulting in the creation of a new self-image.

A Winner's self-talk: "Of course I can do it! I've practiced it mentally a thousand times." Losers say: "How can you expect me to do it? I don't know how!"

Take Action Today for More Positive Self-discipline

1. *Make an appointment to visit one of the following during the next thirty days*—a military aviation flight simulator, an airline pilot training simulator, or a computer simulation game or training facility at a university. Get a current, first-hand experience with current, state-of-the-art simulation.

2. *Purchase and listen to audio cassette tapes on the art of visualization and simulation.* Learn the steps for conditioning your own mind to relax and become most receptive to your own self-talk. Record your goals in your own voice on an audio cassette. Listen to inspirational music, and play your cassette at the same time softly in the background.

3. *Make a list of five necessary but unpleasant tasks you have been putting off.* Put a completion date after each task. Start and finish each task. Immediate action on unpleasant projects reduces stress and tension.

4. *When you simulate and visualize your goals, visualize the exact achievement* of the specifics as if they had already been accomplished. In other words—Weight: 170 pounds for a man, maybe 115 pounds for a woman and looking trim and firm in a bathing suit or tennis outfit.

5. *As a daily exercise, you should rehearse every important goal achievement simulation* over and over in your imagination like a television football instant replay, as if you had already mastered that act.

6. *After every important performance in your life, whether it's closing a sale, speaking in front of a group, communicating with employees, playing a sport, or dealing with loved ones—you should control your self-talk* to elevate your best self-image of a winning performance. If you performed well, your self-talk should be "That's more like me." If you performed badly, your immediate self-talk should be "That's not like me, I perform better than that." Then you should replay the action correctly in your imagination.

7. *The best times to simulate goals are free, relaxed times—* those few early minutes, upon awakening in the morning each day. In the bath or shower. An excellent time is during automobile or other vehicle commuting trips during which our minds are very close to being "in neutral." During lunch, if we're alone. On a morning, afternoon or evening stroll. And, the very best time, at night in an easy chair or bed during the "twilight minutes" just prior to sleep.

8. *Be relentless and persistent* in your rehearsing of your goal achievements. Both Losing and Winning are learned habits. It takes days and weeks of constant practice to overcome old entrenched attitudes and lifestyles.

9. *Discipline your body to relax and relieve stress* by engaging in some form of "ball-playing" as a routine. This means handball, racquetball, tennis, golf, punching bag, or something involving physical impact. This helps relieve built up internal stress.

10. *Discipline your body to improve your cardiovascular system by jogging or walking* at least three times per week. Optimum distance would be 12 to 18 miles per week. And eat nutritional, balanced meals instead of junk food.

To Win each day
Make it your goal
To play it like
The Superbowl!
Focus all your energy
On what and who
You want to be.

CHAPTER 9

POSITIVE SELF-DIMENSION

Antonyms:
Shallowness, egocentricity, superficiality

Synonyms:
Total person, visionary, humanist

Losers' Self-talk:
"Do it to others before they do it to you."

Winners' Self-talk:
"I am in harmony with the nature and spirit of life and I value you as a person and myself."

Proverb:
"If I can help you win, then I win. If nature wins, everyone wins!"

The real Winners in the game of life have *Positive Self-dimension*.

They look beyond themselves for meaning in life.

Winners put it all together as "A Total Person." What a rare human being—a whole, total person.

Self-dimension takes the Psychology of Winning beyond the self and into the universe.

The greatest example of self-dimension a Winner can display is the quality of earning the love and respect of other human beings.

Winning self-dimension does not mean standing victoriously over a fallen enemy.

Winning self-dimension is extending a strong hand to one who is reaching, or groping or just trying to hang on. Winners know that there will be no lasting peace on Earth until there's a piece of bread in every mouth.

Winners create other winners without exploiting them.

They know that true immortality for the human race is when a caring, sharing person helps even one other individual to live a better life.

Self-dimension starts with the inner circle—the family. Is your family a winning team or a regiment that the kids can hardly wait to grow out of?

Are your marriage and friendships precious? Or have you lost touch except for holidays, anniversaries, reunions, and parties?

Winners get it together with their loved ones, their friends, and with the community in which they live. They also love their careers, but are not married to them. Winners vote and care about the government of their cities, states and nation, and its effectiveness, fairness and honesty. And that of other nations, too.

Winners live a well-rounded life. They build their spheres of relationships with evenly distributed emphasis.

Are you a financial success, with plenty of money to spend, but no time left for your kids? Losers try to buy love and trust, and they always fail.

Do you spend all your time on your family, but not enough time earning enough to care for them?

Do you have a winning scout troop as an outside activity, but a losing, neglected family on the inside?

Are you pretty or macho externally and shallow and egotistical internally?

Does your sphere of life have all the pressure in one point? If it does, it could burst.

Losers in life have the philosophy of "Do it to others before they do it to you." They have the I win and you lose attitude.

Winners practice the Double Win Attitude. "If I help you win, then I win. I win and you win, too!"

And they realize that it's not nice to fool Mother Nature either. Nature is innocent, abundant—but unforgiving.

We have exploited her resources and she's responding like a mirror, reflecting our gluttony and plunder with dwindling resources, pollution, unclean air, unsafe water, toxic food, and cancerous by-products of technology.

As we change our environment to suit our short-range ambitions, we risk the very survival of the human race.

Positive Self-dimension is understanding the vulnerability of the life process and the delicate balance of ecology.

Winners remember those who owned the earth for thousands of years and who are now in the Hall of Fame of the Extinct.

They know that New York could become Tyrannosaurus Rex and Los Angeles the Mastodon unless they cherish the natural environment and put back into Earth at least as much as they take out.

And Winners take their cues from their friends, the animals. They know what sealskin coats and fancy furs of ocelot can mean to future generations.

Someday when Sea World's long gone dry, and all the birds have flown, and all the fish are gone or on your dinner table, and all the animals are rubberized or polyester foam, available exclusively on stage at Disney World—someday a group of wise men will deduce and calculate, that what befell the animals may well be human fate.

Someday, if we're not careful, we may find in some museum, a glass display that lights up when you press the rail, complete with tape recorded spiel, that tells in thirty seconds of the day when man too, roamed the Planet Earth, with his beloved friends—the animals.

Self-dimension—fitting in—drawing upon the spiritual power woven intricately into every fiber of our being.

Winners go beyond the horoscopes and stars and fortune tellers' prophecies, beyond the do-it-to-yourself advice, beyond the plastic surgeon's knife—and live each precious, golden day as if it were their last, building for the future, learning from the past.

When you look in the mirror, whom do you see? Do you see someone you'd like to know? Do you see someone your parents wanted you to be, someone your teachers, your minister, your boss, your husband or your wife, or your friends wanted you to be? When you look in the mirror, do you ever see anyone that *you* wanted you to be?

To the winning girl or woman of today, her Positive Self-dimension might try to say:

Mirror, mirror on my wall
What's the meaning of it all
Is there something more to life
Than to be a loving wife?

Yes, I love my children dearly
But they'll grow up and come by yearly.
Dare I yearn for something more
Than to cook and wax the floor?

What about the needs I feel—
Are my dreams considered real?
What about an education and
A voice to shape our nation?

What about a new profession instead
Of reading True Confession?
I'm not angry or rebelling, but there's
Something strong, compelling.

Is my destined heritage,
Still a two-fold color page
In some Playboy magazine
Just a sexy pin-up queen?

Mirror, mirror on my wall
Help me, help him hear my call
All I've ever hoped to be is
Free—to be that person me.

And for the winning male, here's Self-dimension you
might think about:

Crystal ball, oh crystal ball
Will my empire rise and fall

Like the Roman legions must
Ash to ash, dust to dust?

Is there something more to life
Than to build it for my wife
And to give our children more
Than their parents had before?

Go to work, earn the bread
Watch TV, go to bed
Sunrise, sunset year to year
Before I know it winter's here.

It's no scrimmage, no practice game
And there's no martyr's hall of fame
Time, the speedster, takes its toll
And every day's my Superbowl.

Losers live in classic style
In the never-world of "Someday I'll"
They blame bad luck each time they lose
And hide with sickness, drugs and booze.

Losing's a habit, so is winning
The way to change is by beginning
To live each day, as if my last
Not in the future, nor in the past.

To want it now, to dream it now
To plan it now, to do it now
To close my eyes and clearly see
That person I'd most like to be.

Crystal ball, oh crystal ball
Help me hear my inner call
I think I can, I know I can
Become my greatest coach and fan.

And love myself, and give away
All the love I can today
I think I can, I know I can
Become a most uncommon man.

The television dramatization *Holocaust* reminded us of one of the most infamous self-made men who nearly ruled the world by using self-motivation and self-direction to achieve his goals—but who became the biggest Loser in history—Adolf Hitler. When he was a paperhanger, he convinced a few loyal followers that he was destined to be the ruler of the Third Reich. He used a distorted self-image and relentless self-discipline of simulating his victories, and exuded a fanatic self-confidence that he projected to the masses in Germany through the microphone with methodically calculated words that fanned the fires of hatred and self-expectancy of his people to the deep down belief in ultimate conquest of the free world. He won every battle at the expense of other human beings and lost the ball game in the end, becoming one of the greatest tragedies in modern history, along with millions of men, women and children.

Adolf Hitler was a pathetic example of a "do-it-for-myself" philosophy. He actually had an extremely low self-image and low self-esteem. Traits which seem to be prevalent in all those who yell the loudest and try to focus attention on themselves in a desperate attempt to gain external worthiness to make up for internal neuroses and psychoses.

Positive Self-dimension is being in harmony with the divine order that shapes the entire universe. It is seeing the perfection and beauty manifested by God in nature and accepting the imperfection in man's attempt to reshape nature in his own image, to rationalize his ignorance of the wisdom and intelligence behind life and Creation.

Winners are able to put their own being in dimension with other human beings who lived upon earth nearly one million years before, and are open to the idea that other forms of life, possibly more advanced, may be present in the outer regions of infinity beyond the Palomar telescope and the Apollo and Discoverer space programs.

Winners with Positive Self-dimension, most importantly, have a keen awareness of the value of time, which once spent, is gone from their lives forever. Winners seem to understand a concept which I call "Close Encounters of the *Fourth* Kind." "Close Encounters of the Fourth Kind" have nothing to do with UFO's, Star Wars' fantasies or inter-galactic travel. The Fourth Dimension is time. And time is forever the ruler of each of our lives.

When we were children, time stood still. It took forever for Christmas and summer vacation to arrive. A day in grammar school seemed like a week. Our senior year in high school moved at a turtle's pace. Our twenty-first birth-day was always way out in the future. A Saturday at the beach lasted forever.

"A Close Encounter of the Fourth Kind" is a life expe-rience in which you come face to face with the dramatic reality that there are no time-outs, no substitutions, and no replays in the game of life—and the sobering understanding that the clock is always running. Your encounter may be a near miss on the freeway, the loss of a friend or loved one, a war-time experience, a lengthy illness, or a visit to the burn ward at the intensive care unit at your hospital. Your encounter may be as subtle as a high school class reunion, or the discovery in the attic of old photographs of you and your family. It may be the chance meeting of an "old" friend. Your encounter may be an innocent glance in the bathroom mirror.

Winners learn from their "Close Encounters" and develop a cherished respect for the value of time. Losers begin to fear the passing of time, chasing it, squandering it and, most of all, trying to hide from it beneath a superficial cosmetic veil.

I wrote a simple verse which describes my understanding of my own mortality on the earth:

There isn't more to life than this—
A baby's smile, a loved one's kiss
A book, a song, a flower, a friend
And just a little time—to spend.

Winners understand the mortality of their bodies and are able to age gracefully as a result. They tend their "gardens" like sensitive horticulturists instead of one-shot profit planters. They do not necessarily accept death as the final gun in the game of life. They see it as a transition into another plane which, although they may never come to fully comprehend its meaning while living, they do not fear.

Winners take time to look—at the rosebuds opening each day.

Winners take time to listen—knowing there may be fewer robins next spring.

They take time for children—too soon they fly like arrows from the bow.

They take time to play—knowing that when children grow up they get old.

They take time for old people—knowing that old people live for the next visit from a loved one.

They take time for their families—knowing they are the precious Inner Circle.

They take time for nature—knowing they can't put it on their Master Charge cards.

They take time for animals—knowing it's their world, too.

They take time to read—knowing that good books are a transport of wisdom that can take them to places they can't always visit in person.

Winners take time to work—knowing they can't enjoy

the view unless they climb the mountain.

Winners take time for their health—knowing it's the commodity that they don't recognize and appreciate until they have it no longer.

Winners don't live their lives in the past, becoming senile. They learn from it, not repeating their mistakes but savoring each memory that brought them happiness.

Winners don't live their lives in the distant future, safely out of sight. They set goals in the specific, foreseeable future—which give their everyday activities richness and purpose.

Winners live in the present, in that only moment of time over which they have any control—now—and it's history—now—and it's gone. Winners don't try to buy everything they see, using plastic credit cards in a frantic, hedonistic attempt to do it all now and die with a young body.

I would like to run a classified ad in every newspaper in the world under Lost and Found: "Lost—one twenty-four hour, twenty-four carat, golden day—each hour studded with sixty diamond minutes—each minute studded with sixty ruby seconds. But don't bother to look for it, it's gone forever—that wonderful, golden day, I lost today." Life is not a race to come in first, but one to make last and best. True self-dimension—in the Psychology of Winning in life—is to live every minute as if it were your last—to always look for good—and to cherish the minutes and the lives that you encounter within it.

For each of us, the clock is running. It's no scrimmage— it's not a drill—it's the Superbowl—every day.

There is still plenty of time to Win . . .

But not a minute to Lose!

REVIEW

(Read this Positive Self-dimension Review several times over the period of one month to etch it in your memory.)

Winners see their total person in such a fully-formed perspective that they literally become part of the "big picture" of life—and it of them. They have learned to know themselves intimately. They have learned to see themselves through the eyes of others. They have learned to feel as one with nature and the universe. And they have learned to be aware of time—their opportunity to learn from the past, plan for the future, and live as fully as possible in the present. Winners create other Winners without exploiting them. Winners get it together with their loved ones, their friends, and with the community in which they live. Winners practice the Double-win attitude: "If I help you win, then I win." Positive self-dimension is understanding the vulnerability of the life process and the delicate balance of ecology. Self-dimension—fitting in—drawing upon the spiritual power woven intricately into every fiber of our being. Winners understand the mortality of their bodies, and as a result are able to age gracefully. They do not necessarily accept death as the final gun in the game of life. They see it as a transition which, although they may never come to fully comprehend its meaning, they do not fear; they anticipate its eventual arrival. Winners plant shade trees under which they know they'll never sit. A Winner's self-talk: "I live every moment, enjoying as much, relating as much, doing as much, giving as much as I possibly can." Losers say: "I'm only concerned with me today."

Take Action Today for More Positive Self-dimension:

1. *Ask yourself the questions, how do I fit* into my family, my company, my profession, my community, my nation, my world?

2. *Treat people more like brothers and sisters.* Treat animals more like people. Treat nature more carefully and tenderly—she is precariously balancing our future survival.

3. *Pay value to your spouse or loved one today* with a touch and an "I love you." Flowers, poems, cards are ever green!

4. *Tonight kiss a child goodnight with an added, "You are special* and I love you for who you are." And tomorrow listen to and play with that child as if you were a playmate again.

5. *Tell a parent or relative in person or by phone how much he or she means to you today.*

6. *Spend time listening to and giving encouragement to an elder* each week.

7. *Make a contribution to something or someone for which there is no direct payoff or obligation.*

8. *This Saturday do something you have wanted to do for years.* And repeat this process once each month.

9. *Experiment with five or six hours sleep per night* while being kind to your body with good nutrition and exercise. Over a lifetime, the additional productive hours available amount to 12 more years of life.

10. *Learn one or two additional languages* and study the customs and mores of countries you plan to visit. When you travel, speak in the native tongue as much as possible. The added dimension will benefit you and those you meet.

Success Formula
Conceive + Believe = Achieve
Visualize + Internalize = Realize
Imagination + Simulation =
  Realization

CHAPTER **10** _____

POSITIVE
SELF-PROJECTION

Antonyms:
Aloof, unfriendly, unkempt

Synonyms:
Personable, supportive, impressive

Losers' Self-talk:
"Don't confuse me with facts, my mind's made up."

Winners' Self-talk:
"Tell me more of your needs."

Proverb:
"How you walk, talk, listen, and look is You!"

Winners in life are walking examples of *Positive Self-projection*.

You can always spot a Winner when he or she first enters a room.

Winners project an aura; they have an unmistakable presence; they have a charisma which is disarming, radiating and magnetic. They project that warm glow that comes from inside out.

Most importantly, Winners are naturally open and friendly. They know that a smile is the universal language that opens doors, melts defenses and saves a thousand words. A smile is the light in your window that tells others there is a caring, sharing person inside.

Winners are aware that first impressions are powerful and create lasting attitudes. They understand that interpersonal relationships can be won or lost in about the first four minutes of conversation.

Winners have learned through experience that—fairly or unfairly—people project and respond to a visceral or "gut level" feeling which is nearly instantaneous.

Many careers, top jobs, sales and other important transactions are decided very early in the interview or negotiation.

Winners know that everyone projects and receives through a different encoding and decoding system... as if each of us had his own CB radio with no one else tuned in on his exact frequency.

Therefore, Winners in life realize that the best they can hope for in the communication process with others is for a common level of general understanding.

There are some fundamental, consistent patterns that winning human beings follow in Positive Self-projection:

First, Winners always look like Winners at their best. They know that the clock is running, that the bird of time is on the wing and they feel that, since there is no time to lose, why not put their best foot forward.

Winners respect the fact that we as people, usually project on the outside how we really feel about ourselves on the inside. For example, when we aren't feeling well physically, we don't look well at the skin or surface level. And correspondingly, when we don't feel good about ourselves emotionally or mentally, we don't seem to make a very good impression with our looks, personal grooming and clothing habits.

Studies have shown the definite correlation between looking good and success in life. A recent Harvard study pointed out that people who feel unattractive, as judged by themselves and their peers, tend to suffer from feelings of loneliness, rejection and isolation. School children who look good are actually treated better not only by their classmates, but by teachers as well. The term good looking as we are using it, does not necessarily mean beautiful or handsome like a movie star because other studies have shown that some of the most beautiful young people physically are less satisfied, less well-adjusted and less happy in later life.

What can we learn from these insights? First, while we have no choice over the genes we have inherited, and thus are stuck with our general shape, structure and skin . . . it is to our advantage to take care of our health and appearance and to do what we can to enhance what we've got, because like it or not, we will usually be judged by our looks in an instant and lasting impression. And secondly, since we behave according to the way we *think* we look, rather than the way we *actually* look to others, those of us who can learn to be fairly satisfied with our features are way ahead of the game as far as being Winners in life.

In today's cosmetic society there is a real need for rational values when we consider the true meaning of Positive Self-projection.

We seem to be taking a good thing, which is "doing the best with what we've got," and going overboard with excessive self-adoration and self-indulgence in an attempt to buy the fountain of youth and superficial happiness. We know, of course, that the kind of house, car, clothing, and possessions we show off to the world represent our attempt to tell others who we are.

More important than telling others who we are, is that our expressed standards of living serve to remind us *ourselves* who we are. In today's world of easy credit—in what some have called the "plastic age" because of the flood of credit cards and the ease with which they can be obtained and used—almost anyone can arrange to display a Cadillac or power boat or motor home in front of his house. Therefore, as was referred to earlier in the chapter on self-esteem, the tendency to show off many toys and trappings of affluence and material success is more likely to say to others that we are really lacking in self-esteem or self-worth than the fact that we can afford it. It is fair to say that only an individual who has a strong sense of self-respect can afford to project a modest image to the community.

In other words, Winners can project success without flaunting it. Winners may not always be able to afford to buy the most expensive things, but they always do the very best with what they can afford.

So we don't have to be rich or spend a fortune to project the look of a Winner. All it takes is a little extra effort and time in personal grooming. A good appearance is the way to stop people who are important to us and gain their attention long enough to project our inside value, like a good book among the thousands available on the bookstore shelf.

Another important point in winning self-projection, is the way in which we introduce ourselves to others. It sounds so basic, almost silly. Winners—in a first encounter, whether in person or by telephone—usually lead by giving their own name first. "Hello, my name is Denis Waitley." As simple as it may seem, by stating our own name up front in a positive, affirmative manner, we are projecting self-worth and giving others immediate reason to accept us as someone important to remember.

Winners get in touch by extending their hand first, knowing that it is the time-proven way of paying value to others. And along with the warm handshake, Winners use direct eye contact and a warm, open smile to project interest in communication.

Nothing marks a Loser so clearly as shifty, wandering eyes—unable to look straight into our own, but looking down and away as if to say, "I can't be straightforward with you because it's too uncomfortable."

And nothing marks a Winner so clearly as a relaxed smile and a face that volunteers his own name and enjoys it, while extending his hand to yours, and looking directly into your eyes.

Winners learn the art of projecting themselves through active listening. Once they introduce themselves they become listeners. They know that listeners learn a great deal while talkers learn nothing. Winners ask questions, they draw the other person out, they ask for examples, they ask others to put it in other words and they feed back what others have just said for clarity and understanding. Winners know that paying value to others is the greatest communication skill of all.

Earl Nightingale, one of the greatest self-development

philosophers of our time, calls this skill the "I'll make him glad he talked with me" attitude. This great idea is so simple it's almost deceptive. We have to examine it carefully to understand how it works and why.

"I'll make him glad" is an attitude that can become a whole way of life.

When a Winner faces a prospect, an adversary or a potential friend, or when he picks up a telephone, his attitude is service-oriented, not self-oriented. His concern is for the other person, not himself.

When we have someone else's interest at heart, not just our own, the other person can sense it. He may not be able to put into words why he feels that way, but he does. On the other hand, people get an uneasy feeling when they talk with a person who has only his own interests in mind and not theirs.

There's an excellent reason why we all get these feelings about people. It's known as nonverbal communication. It's the old business of "What you are speaks so loudly, I can't hear what you are saying." And it's tremendously important to all of us.

In his book, *Nonverbal Communications*, Dr. Jurgen Ruesch, Professor of Psychiatry at the University of California, says that we communicate by means of some seven hundred thousand nonverbal signals! Now when we consider the limited vocabulary of the average person, it's easy to understand why nonverbal communication has more effect than most of us realize.

People, whether they know it or not, telegraph their intentions and feelings. Whatever goes on on the inside shows on the outside. We receive most of these nonverbal communications below the conscious level of thinking. Our subconscious, robot-like minds evaluate them and serve them up to us as "feelings" based on past experience.

When we adopt the "I'll make him glad he talked with me" attitude—the idea of helping the other person solve his problem—we have his interest at heart. Then the feelings he receives agree with what he hears us say and the climate is right for us both to benefit. Everybody wins with this attitude.

Winners listen to the total person. They observe body language, realizing that folded or crossed arms sometimes mean a defensive or introverted listener. They understand that hands on the hips or active gesturing can mean an aggressive attitude.

Winners watch the eyes which can look down or away in self-consciousness or guilt or which can flare or pinpoint in surprise or anger. Winners listen to the extra-verbal messages. The tone of voice. The tremor. The nervous laugh. The rehearsed, unemotional monotone or the drama of the obvious or subtle actor.

Winners in business, personal relationships and in marriage, take full responsibility for success in the communication process. In other words, Winners never meet you half-way or go fifty-fifty. As listeners, Winners take full responsibility for hearing what you mean. As talkers, Winners take full responsibility for being certain that you understand what they are saying. By giving examples, by asking you for feedback, by putting what they said in different words, they make it easy for you to gain the true intent of their communication.

And, Winners use the KISS formula. KISS in communications means "Keep It Straightforward and Simple." Winners know that everyone interprets what he hears and sees differently. Winners project in clear, concise, simple language and use words and examples that don't evoke a double meaning or hidden agenda.

And last, and most important—Winners in life project constructive, supportive ideas. Winners are neither cynical nor critical. Winners accept another viewpoint as being valid even if it is diametrically opposed to their own beliefs. A Winner says, "I appreciate and understand your position—

however, I may feel differently and, if so, I would like to tell you why my position may be different from your own."

When Will Rogers said, "I never met a man I didn't like," I'm sure he didn't mean he approved of all the traits and characteristics of every person he met. But he found something he could admire in everyone. We get back from people what we give them. If we want to be loved, we must first be lovable.

Think back to the people who have had the most influence on you. You'll likely find that they were people who really cared about you—your parents, a fine teacher, a business associate, a good friend—someone who was interested in you. And the only people you will influence to any great degree will be the people you care about. When you are with people you care about their interest, not yours, will be uppermost in your mind. This is most evident in marriage and parenthood, but it's also true in every other area of our lives. It has been said that, "Marriage is not looking at each other, but looking in the same direction together." And this is just as applicable to other aspects of life as it is to marriage. "It's not looking at each other, but looking in the same direction together."

Our success in getting along with others and communicating effectively with them depends upon this same principle. It depends solely upon our ability to help other people solve their problems.

This is winning self-projection. Winners say, "I'll make you glad you talked with me." And you'll know you're a true Winner in the game of life when you hear this statement often from those you meet: "I like me best when I'm with you."

Let's win together by helping each other. Project yourself every day as a Winner, because . . . There is no time to Lose.

REVIEW

(Read this Positive Self-projection Review several times over the period of one month to etch it in your memory.)

Winners practice *Positive Self-projection*. They project their best selves every day in the way they look, walk, talk, listen, and react. They specialize in truly effective communication, taking one hundred per cent of the responsibility not only for sending information or telling, but also for receiving information or listening for the real meaning from every person they contact. Winners are aware that first impressions are powerful, and that interpersonal relationships can be won or lost in about the first four minutes of conversation. Winners say "I'll make them glad they talked with me." To a Winner you'll say "I like me best when I'm with you." Nothing marks a Winner so clearly as a relaxed smile and a warm face that volunteers his or her own name, while extending a hand to yours, looking directly in your eyes, and showing interest in you by asking questions about your life which are important to you. Winners know that paying value to others is the greatest communication skill of all. A Winner's self-talk: "Tell me what you want, maybe we can work on it together." Losers say: "There's no point in discussing it, we're not even on the same wave length."

Take Action Today for
More Positive Self-projection:

1. *Project Positive Self-awareness*. Observe the wonder and abundance in nature. Stop feeling sorry for yourself. If you are alive and enjoy some degree of health, you've got it made. Try looking at yourself through others' eyes.

2. *Project Positive Self-esteem*. Get that deep down feeling of your own worth and pass it along to others. Talk yourself and others up.

3. *Project Positive Self-control*. Project an image of responsibility by making your own luck through preparation and affirmative action.

4. *Project Positive Self-motivation*. Motivate yourself and others by focusing on the rewards of success, forgetting the penalties of failure.

5. *Project Positive Self-expectancy*. Your enthusiasm will be wonderfully contagious and infect almost everyone it touches.

6. *Project a Positive Self-image*. Project your creative imagination and always present a positive preview of your coming attractions with vivid descriptions.

7. *Project Positive Self-direction*. Put your goals down on paper and share them with those who can help you achieve them.

8. *Project Positive Self-discipline*. Talk to yourself over and over again when you are relaxed, visualizing yourself in the act of enjoying and completing each of your current goals. Complete the projects you begin.

9. *Project Positive Self-dimension*. Project yourself as a Winner who creates other Winners too.

10. *Project Positive Self-projection*. Don't just read The Psychology of Winning as another book. Go out and do it!

"The only limits
To my accomplishments
In life . . .
Are self-imposed."

WRAPUP

Your Psychology of Winning

The Psychology of Winning in life is developing a lifestyle that is pleasing and inspiring to yourself and at the same time sets a healthy example for those who look to you for guidance and encouragement in their own lives.

The key is projecting that image of yourself that you would most like to become and practicing on a daily basis.

Since all losing habits such as self-criticism, smoking, excessive drinking, overeating, laziness, anxiety, depression, sloppiness, dishonesty, cruelty, and insensitivity are learned and developed into character traits through relentless practice—so are winning habits learned and retained.

The Winners in life begin by fantasizing their own "scripts," as if their lives were a magnificent, epic motion picture for which they have been chosen as writer, producer, director, and star.

When you project the Ten Qualities of a Total Winner into your own life, they can become your own Ten Commandments for personal growth and achievement of your own individual definition of success.

Begin by projecting #1., *Positive Self-awareness*. Step back from your own life and take a long walk on the beach or in the woods, or by a lake, or up a mountain trail. Observe the wonder and abundance in nature. Make an honest assessment of what you are doing, where you are going, and who you are becoming. Understand the marvel of your own uniqueness and, in a moment of truth, realize how you have

been selling yourself short across the board in evaluating
your own potential. Stop feeling sorry for yourself. If you
are alive and enjoy some degree of health, you've got it
made. As you consider the other human beings who influence your life, try feeling "where they are coming from,"
before passing judgment. Try looking at yourself through
their eyes.

Next, Project #2., *Positive Self-esteem.* Even if it feels
uncomfortable, accept all the compliments, gifts and values
offered by others for whatever reason they offer them by
simply saying, "Thank you." Get that deep down inside
feeling of your own worth. Accept yourself as an imperfect,
but growing individual. Give yourself your own love so you
can give it away, and share as much of it as you can with
others. Be proud of your own accomplishments and goals.
And talk yourself up as a Winner every day of your life.
Your Robot is listening!

Project yourself as one who exercises #3., *Positive Self-
control.* Know that you are responsible for causing your
own effects, that *you* make it happen and that life is a do-
it-to-yourself project. Take advantage of the many choices
and alternatives available to you in your everyday decisions.
Realize that you make your own luck by preparation and
affirmative action. Learn how to relax your body and gain
control of body functions (which you thought were involuntary) by employing new biofeedback, relaxation response
or meditation techniques coupled with a nutritional diet and
exercise program.

The projection of the first three traits should lead you
automatically to #4., *Positive Self-motivation.* When you
see your potential, feel deserving and know that you are in
charge, you get that itch to get going. Remember that you
are becoming what you are thinking about every waking
moment—so it is important to motivate yourself and others
close to you by focusing on desire instead of fear. While
the stresses of fear cause anxiety, neuroses, ulcers, and

disease, the stresses of desire provide energy, propulsion, creativity, and magnetic pull.

When you are motivated and moving forward, it is important to project the most outwardly identifiable characteristic of a winner, trait #5., *Positive Self-expectancy*. Be optimistic about yourself. Develop a true understanding of psychosomatic medicine and the fact that, to a degree, you create your own horoscope and luck. What you expect to happen, with deep conviction and emotion, can surely come to pass. Enthusiasm is wonderfully contagious, infecting almost everyone it touches.

Project your creative imagination with #6., *Positive Self-image*. Remember, when you set your subconscious Robot achievement mechanism high, your behavior and performance will automatically seek that level. What you see with words, pictures and emotions is what you'll get. Understand that your Robot's tape program can never be erased, but that new images can be superimposed over the old ones. Also, comprehend the significance in the knowledge that the subconscious, Robot level of thinking cannot tell the difference between that which is really happening and that which is being rehearsed and synthetically experienced. Therefore, your imagination rules your world!

Project purpose into your life by practicing #7., *Positive Self-direction*. Remember that the mind is a magnificent bio-computer that functions in very specific terms to very specific kinds of data instructions. Set a game plan for your life with worthwhile goals that are incremental and realistic. Put your goals down on paper and define monthly targets and daily tasks. Know that your Robot subconscious is like an automatic pilot that will seek any target you set, but without a goal will cause your system to wander aimlessly around or even self-destruct.

When you have set goals and are committed to their achievement, you need to project yourself as an individual who is dedicated to #8., *Positive Self-discipline*. Real self-discipline is achievement simulation or the ability to practice within, when you are without. Losing is a developed habit and so is winning. Winners simulate success in specific practiced role-playing as if it had already happened. Talk to yourself over and over again when you are relaxed, visualizing yourself in the act of enjoying and completing each of your current goals. Visualization + Internalization = Realization—is an equation you should use the rest of your life!

As you simulate your goals week after week and enjoy the exhilaration of their accomplishment, you will be able to gain character as to the real values in your life by projecting trait #9., *Positive Self-dimension.* Project yourself as a Total Winner who wins at home, professionally, in the community, in the nation, among all people and in the universe, both natural and spiritual. Earn the respect of other human beings. While you are winning, create other Winners, too. Do your business to the benefit of others, not at their expense. Practice the Double-win! Stop procrastinating your fulfillment. Make someday become now!

And, when you're projecting #10., *Positive Self-projection,* understand that you, yourself are no more than the composite picture of all your thoughts and actions. In your relationships with others, there's a basic and critically important rule: "If you want to be loved, be lovable. If you want respect, set a respectable example!" As long as change is inevitable, why not play your hand to win? You can't change the heredity or the early environment you were dealt. But you certainly can change your attitude toward them and learn how to respond to life in a healthier, happier and more worthwhile manner.

There are literally thousands of self-help programs and books today, each with a different formula for self-actualization and individual happiness. They range from Dale Carnegie, to *Your Erroneous Zones* to Pyramid Power to est and from intimidation, to meditation, to religion.

The books each contain words of authors who were inspired to share their thoughts. You alone, the reader, give the message life. You turn the pages. You react, compare, recall, and respond. You close the book when you are through. Whether you put it back on the shelf or pass it along to someone who may enjoy it or need it—usually you continue your established ways and do little about incorporating some of the good points from the book into your own life.

So here is one called *The Psychology of Winning*. So now you've read it—go out and do it!

BIBLIOGRAPHY

Allen, James, *As a Man Thinketh*. New York: Grosset & Dunlap, Inc., 1959; Lakemont, Ga.: CSA Press, new edition, 1975, softcover.

Berne, Eric. *Beyond Games and Scripts: Selections from His Major Writings*. Edited by Claude Steiner and Carmen Kerr. New York: Grove Press, Inc., 1976; Grove Press, Inc., 1977, paperback.

———. *Games People Play: The Psychology of Human Relationships*. New York: Grove Press, Inc., 1964; Grove Press, Inc., 1964, paperback; Random House, Inc., Ballantine Books, Inc., 1976, paperback.

The Bible.

Briggs, Dorothy Corkille. *Your Child's Self-Esteem: The Key to His Life*. New York: Doubleday & Co., Inc., 1970; Doubleday & Co., Inc., Dolphin Books, 1975, paperback.

Bristol, Claude. *The Magic of Believing*. Englewood Cliffs, N.J.: Prentice-Hall, Inc., 1957; New York: Cornerstone Library, Inc., 1967, paperback.

Carnegie, Dale. *How to Win Friends and Influence People*. New York: Simon & Schuster, Inc., 1936; Pocket Books, Inc., 1977, paperback.

Frankl, Viktor E. *Man's Search for Meaning*. Revised edition. Boston, Mass.: Beacon Press, Inc., 1963; New York: Pocket Books, Inc., 1975, paperback.

Fromm, Erich. *The Art of Loving*. New York: Harper & Row Publishers, Inc., Perennial Library, 1974, paperback.

Gardiner, John W. *Excellence: Can We Be Equal and Excellent Too*. New York: Harper & Row Publishers, Inc., 1961; Harper & Row Publishers, Inc., Perennial Library, 1971, paperback.

_____. *Self-Renewal: The Individual and the Innovative Society*. New York: Harper & Row Publishers, Inc., 1964; Harper & Row Publishers, Inc., Colophon Books, 1964, paperback; Harper & Row, Publishers, Inc., Perennial Library, 1971, paperback.

Gibran, Kahlil. *The Prophet*. New York: Alfred A. Knopf, Inc., 1923.

Glasser, William, M.D. *Schools Without Failure*. New York: Harper & Row Publishers, Inc., 1969; Harper & Row Publishers, Inc., Perennial Library, 1975, paperback.

Harris, Thomas A., M.D. *"I'm OK—You're OK: A Practical Guide to Transactional Analysis*. New York: Harper & Row Publishers, Inc., 1969; Avon Books, 1973, paperback.

Hill, Napoleon. *Think and Grow Rich*. New York: Hawthorne Books, Inc., 1966; Fawcett World Library, 1976, paperback.

Hoffer, Eric. *The True Believer*. New York: Harper & Row Publishers, Inc., 1951; Harper & Row Publishers, Inc., Perennial Library, 1966, paperback.

James, Muriel, and Jongeward, Dorothy. *Born to Win: Transactional Analysis with Gestalt Experiments*. Reading, Mass.: Addison-Wesley Publishing Co., Inc., 1971.

Lao Tzu. *Tao Te Ching*. Translated by D. C. Lau. New York: Penguin Books, Inc., 1964, paperback.

Lederer, William J., and Jackson, Don D. *The Mirages of Marriage*. New York: W. W. Norton & Company, Inc., 1968.

Lindbergh, Anne Morrow. *Gift from the Sea*. New York: Pantheon Books, 1955; Random House, Inc., Vintage Trade Books, 1965, paperback.

Maltz, Maxwell, M.D. *Psycho-Cybernetics: The New Way to a Successful Life*. Englewood Cliffs, N.J.: Prentice-Hall, Inc., 1960; Pocket Books, Inc., paperback.

Maslow, Abraham H. *The Farther Reaches of Human Nature*. New York: Viking Press, Inc., 1971.

Nightingale, Earl. *This Is Earl Nightingale*. New York: Doubleday & Co., Inc., 1969.

Osborn, Alex F. *Applied Imagination: Principles and Procedures of Creative Problem-Solving*. 3rd edition. New York: Charles Scribner's Sons, 1963, paperback.

Selye, Hans. *Stress Without Distress*. Philadelphia: J. B. Lippincott Co., 1974; New York: New American Library, Signet Books, 1975, paperback.

ABOUT THE AUTHOR

Dr. Denis Waitley, who holds a doctorate in human behavior, serves on the faculty of the U.S.C. College of Continuing Education and acts as a consultant to corporations, government and private organizations. He appears regularly as a speaker and panelist along with Dr. Norman Vincent Peale, Paul Harvey, William F. Buckley, Jr. and other well-known winners.